AHEAD OF THE CURVE

Nine Simple Ways to Create Wealth by Spotting Stock Trends

HILARY KRAMER

Finance Editor and Money Coach of AOL

FREE PRESS

New York London Toronto Sydney

Note to Readers

This publication contains the opinions and ideas of its author. It is sold with the understanding that neither the author nor the publisher is engaged in rendering legal, tax, investment, financial, accounting, or other professional advice or services. If the reader requires such advice or services, a competent professional should be consulted. Relevant laws vary from state to state. The strategies outlined in this book may not be suitable for every individual, and are not guaranteed or warranted to produce any particular results. No warranty is made with respect to the accuracy or completeness of the information contained herein, and both the author and the publisher specifically disclaim any responsibility for any liability, loss or risk, personal or otherwise, which is incurred as a consequence, directly or indirectly, of the use and application of any of the contents of this book.

fP
FREE PRESS
A Division of Simon & Schuster, Inc.
1230 Avenue of the Americas
New York, NY 10020

First Free Press hardcover edition October 2007

FREE PRESS and colophon are trademarks of Simon & Schuster, Inc.

For information about special discounts for bulk purchases, please contact Simon & Schuster Special Sales at 1-800-456-6798 or business@simonandschuster.com

Designed by Kyoko Watanabe

Manufactured in the United States of America

10 9 8 7 6 5 4 3 2 1

Library of Congress Cataloging-in-Publication Data
Kramer, Hilary.
Ahead of the curve / Hilary Kramer.
1. Investments. 2. Finance, Personal. I. Title.
HG4521.K69 2007
332.6—dc22 2007016368

ISBN-13: 978-1-4165-4685-6
ISBN-10: 1-4165-4685-5

For those who want the freedom that wealth brings:
I hope to inspire you.

Contents

INTRODUCTION

Opportunities for Great Wealth Are Everywhere—You Just Need to See Them

Spotting a reliable stock trend is like surfing a wave. If you've ever watched someone surf—or been lucky enough to surf yourself—you know that most of the time in the water is spent waiting, watching, alert, being "one with nature." What is all the vigilance for? Good surfers wait to spot the perfect wave. When it finally comes, they're able to catch it for a great ride.

Creating wealth is similar. It is all about spotting opportunity, being open to the investment possibilities inherent all around you in your life, and, most important, perceiving a trend *before it becomes a trend*. At just the right time, a perceptive investor jumps on a developing trend like a great wave and surfs it all the way to the bank.

But what exactly are the best trends to jump on right now? If you're looking to find a trend list in this book, you should put it down right now. You won't find me telling you about the trend *du jour*. Consult the latest edition of your favorite TV money show or your favorite financial blog or magazine for that kind of information. But beware. The pundits will most likely be telling you about yesterday's trends. Also, millions of others will be getting that information at the same time. Invest in China! Social networking is the next big thing! Video on Demand will make you rich! The problem with books and pundits telling you about the specific trends of today is that tomorrow these tips will be useless. *The very nature of trends is that they are constantly in flux*. Just as a wave rolls in, then crashes against the shore and is gone forever, if you don't ride a trend at the right moment, you will lose it. I don't want to tell you about a wave that's already crashed. I want this book to teach you a skill that you can use today, tomorrow, and ten years from now.

I'll show you how to spot a reliable emerging trend yourself before the pundits are onto it. I'll help you hone your opportunity-spotting skills, and I'll lay out how you can use trend-spotting techniques to make good money today—and for the rest of your life. I actually prefer to think of trend spotting as a form of spying: constantly looking for clues in places other people don't expect to find them, never letting anything slip by unnoticed, always paying attention to your surroundings.

From the time I was just a kid, selling sunglasses on the boardwalk at the Jersey Shore, to my successful career in money management, to my role as a Financial Life Coach for AOL and a television commentator, I have found that *spotting trends* is the key to becoming rich. You didn't need to go to business school, or to any school for that matter. You don't need to have a sophisticated knowledge of financial models and data. You don't need to have lots of money. It often seems so hard to get rich, but the truth is that you simply need to be able to see a good money opportunity before others do—and jump on it. This book will show you how, and it will show you that you are perfectly capable of doing it yourself. All you need in order to think in a trend-spotting way are the simple techniques that I'll show you.

As you get a feel for these techniques, you will grow more and more comfortable with your ability to see a good wave coming. A confident trend surfer is usually the most successful at making money. As you spend more time surfing, you will make more decisions that pay off, and your confidence will grow. Not every pick will be a winner. The key is not to let your confidence get destroyed by mistakes, and to learn from them instead. And remember: Don't get overconfident! That's a sure way to find yourself wiping out completely.

As you gain confidence, you'll also learn which waves

are the ones you know how to ride. What might seem like a good wave to the next person is not necessarily a good wave for you. Not every investor is the same. High-risk investors are like high-risk surfers: They look for the big waves, dropping into 20-footers by helicopter in Hawaii, taking amazing rides but with equally brutal wipeouts. They ride risky trends, go for broke—and sometimes end up that way. A measured investor, in contrast, rides the 5-footers; some of them are awesome, others fizzle out, but rarely do these surfers completely bite it. And then there are cautious boogie boarders, surfing small waves, never coming up big but almost never getting hurt, either. Knowing your investing style and limitations as you head into the investing game helps you home in on trends you are willing to jump onto—whether risky but potentially incredibly lucrative or very safe but with lesser payout.

My personal investing style isn't that of a hard-core surfer, but I'm also not afraid to catch a fairly big wave when I see it coming. There is no right or wrong investing style, and my intention in this book is not to sell you on one over the other. But understanding your risk tolerance helps you know what kinds of wave you are most comfortable riding and will help you apply the tips I give you. It is also important to remember several points as you home in on your surfing style:

1. *Diversifying is crucial.* No matter what your surfing style, it is important to diversify your investments. Don't pour all your money into the stock market,

even if you are a high-risk surfer. Many investment books provide a formula for how much you should keep in low-risk cash and bond investments versus high-risk stock market investments. I'm not a proponent of one over another, but I am a proponent of spreading your money around—whether in a traditional savings account, stocks, bonds, mutual funds, index funds, real estate trusts (REITs), or any other investment vehicle. Even within stocks, it's wise to diversify among companies in different sectors. Just as you wouldn't have wanted your life savings to be wiped out with the dot-com crash, you should spread your investments across different sectors so you can surf past future wipeouts. Keep some cash for a rainy day, invest some of your money in safer, albeit lower-yielding investments like bonds and certificates of deposit, and if your style permits, put some money in higher-risk stocks.

2. *Don't be afraid to start your own stock portfolio.* Although it is important to diversify your money, if you are able to put some portion of your investing funds into building your own portfolio of individual stocks, the payoffs can well exceed the returns from investing in bonds, CDs, and even stocks owned through mutual funds or index funds. As the Wharton professor Jeremy Siegel points out in his book *Stocks for the Long Run*, stock market returns have averaged more than 14 percent a year since 1982, and they have averaged more than 10 percent a year since 1926. Despite what pro-

fessional money managers out there may tell you, you can do just as well as they, if not better, investing your own money if you know what to look for. Of course they are going to tell you they know better than you, because their jobs depend on people like you giving them your money to invest—and often taking heavy fees off the top. But take a look at the average performance of a mutual fund: the market tends to outperform the fund. This means, if you are investing wisely in the market, you stand a very good chance of making more money than you'd make had you let a professional money manager with a fancy business degree invest it for you.

This should be a fun process—as if you were collecting something like baseball cards. You want to like and understand the companies you invest in. You want to *build* a portfolio made up of stock from individual companies you've picked, as well as from diversified mutual funds or indexes like the S&P 500 or the Russell 2000, or internationally diversified mutual funds that have reduced risk.

3. *Be smart in the amount you put into the stock market.* You don't need to be a millionaire to start out. An investor can start out with $500, $5,000, or $50,000. Although some brokerages have minimums of $2,000, many don't have any minimums at all anymore. My rule of thumb is to be aware that whatever I invest in the market is at risk. Whatever I put in, I have to be willing to lose. Of course, I hope this will never happen

to either of us. But remembering that my invested money is at risk helps me measure the amount that I want to put into the market and the amount I'd rather put into safer investments. It's also important to know that you don't need to dump all your money into a single stock that you think has promise.

Take baby steps in the beginning. If you like a company, invest a few hundred dollars. If things are trending in a positive direction, then pick up some more shares, even if they might be a bit more expensive than the initial investment. The most important point when you are building your own portfolio is . . .

4. *How many should I own?* Often, people who are just building a portfolio for the first time ask me, How many stocks should I include? If you are including in your portfolio diversified mutual funds or index funds, you will automatically own quite a few different stocks. But in terms of the stocks you pick on your own, you can have as few as one stock to as many as thirty. It depends on how much you want to watch them and how much time you have to devote. I personally own ten stocks at a time, never more.

   I like to know what I own, and I take chances that are based on really having conviction about a company and believing that I am ahead of everyone else. Remember, the more stocks you own, the more you have to pay attention to your portfolio, because it's critical that you know what's going on with each. Which means . . .

5. *Always do your homework*. As with all types of investments, don't ride any waves blindly when it comes to stock picking. You must do your homework before putting your money into any company. The first rule of investing in individual stocks is that you've got to be sure to check the company's fundamental financials. I will introduce some ways to do so a little later in the book, and there is no shortage of good information about this on the web and in magazines and books. Don't worry: nothing I ask you to do gets too technical. The basics are really quite easy and not very time intensive, especially given how readily accessible the necessary financial reports are online.
6. *Buy low, sell high*. This rule is the key to trend surfing. Jump in when the wave is just starting, jump off before it crashes. It's obvious, but it bears repeating, and you'll hear it from me again and again in this book. But don't get too obsessed with timing. By this, I mean don't be afraid to jump on a wave because you think it might dip lower first, and don't be afraid to jump off a wave because you fear it might grow a bit more after you've dumped it. As long as you sell higher than you bought, you will end up ahead. (Keep tax considerations in mind, though: Uncle Sam will want a share of your gains.)

   Maybe you'll find you could have surfed the wave a little longer and made more, but don't beat yourself up over it. It's always better to leave a little on the table than to wipe out with less than you put in!

7. *How do you actually buy and sell*? There are many ways the average investor can buy and sell stocks: through brokerages and, now more than ever, online. Do your research about the fees involved. There are many discount brokers today offering free or flat rates. In addition to broker fees, pay attention to possible maintenance fees, custodial fees, and other costs (especially with mutual funds and international funds). When you are selling, be aware of your tax bracket and the tax implications of short-term and long-term gains. You don't want to be surprised when April 15 rolls around and the IRS serves you with a big tax bill.
8. *Think to the future*. It is so easy to get caught up in the "now." So many of us want results *today*, and if we see returns, we want to spend them immediately. But think to tomorrow. Be an investor rather than a day trader. One of the best waves you'll catch is when you buy a stock today that grows because of a future trend. If your homework on the stock tells you so, it can be worthwhile to hold onto some of these for a while. Besides thinking about future trends and the future of your stocks, you also want to think about *your* future. You want to put as much as you can into a retirement account. Whether a Roth, a deductible, or a nondeductible retirement account, an IRA of one kind or another is crucial. There are plenty of reliable books and website articles that will help you choose the best way to invest for retirement, and you should invest being mindful of how far from retirement you are.

9. *Know your time horizon.* Your surfing style should reflect your age to a certain extent. If you are young, you have the luxury of time to think about investing in things with long-term, high-growth potential. You can afford to be a higher-risk surfer and to take a chance on certain types of riskier stocks. You would then be able to hold those stocks through down periods, and even if you wipe out, you can often start over. However, the closer you are to retirement, the more you should be considering putting your money into relatively secure investments. High-risk stock investing can be the path to a difficult old age without money to provide for yourself or your family.
10. *Be patient and vigilant.* Don't expect a stock to take off overnight. If you are putting your money into an IPO (initial public offering of a stock), for instance, it might take some time for the company to grow. If you see promise, and you've done your research and the company is solid, be patient and you'll likely be rewarded. Remember the double-digit returns that stocks have earned over the long haul. Also, be patient with yourself. Allow yourself to make mistakes. Fall in love with the trend-spotting game, but don't fall too closely in love with any of your stocks. Don't forget to keep a close eye on your portfolio. If signs point to one of them taking a turn for the worse, let it go! There will always be another good one that comes your way. And most of all, while you are making money, have fun!

Some reliable sources I often go to for financial information and research:

Magazines like *Smart Money, Fortune, Forbes, Fast Company, BusinessWeek, The Economist*

Newspapers like *The Wall Street Journal, The New York Times* business section, *Financial Times*

Government organizations like the Securities and Exchange Commission (SEC)

Websites of all the above publications, along with Google Finance, AOL Finance, Yahoo! Finance, MSN Money, MarketWatch, CNN Money, Reuters, Motley Fool, Morningstar

I also use alert systems like Google Alerts, where you can have information about specific companies emailed to you whenever they appear in the news.

As AOL's Finance Editor and Money Coach, I provide personal finance advice and inspirational wisdom to anyone looking to turn his or her financial situation around. In this book, I will act as your coach to make you motivated to spy everyday opportunities, be confident to jump on the ones that are right for you, and as I have done so many times, surf these opportunities to big payoffs.

In the following chapters, I'll present nine basic techniques for spotting and riding trends. I'll also tell the stories of lots of trends—and how my small and large investments paid off. This has worked for me, and I've seen it work for many others, like the teacher who thought that Price Club (now Costco) was a revolutionary way to shop and, building a portfolio on that vision, is worth $5 million today, and the mechanic who noticed that Toyotas really don't break down and bought the stock at $50 in 2002, then rode it to $120.

I'll include plenty of my own stories as well. There is a reason that I get hired to provide financial advice. I've made good millions and was able to retire at thirty-seven years of age following the methods I'll present, and those who have followed my advice have done very well too. I spotted the coming cell phone era and bought Qualcomm stock early, watching it go up 3,000 percent. I invested $27,000 in three thousand shares of Univision, the Spanish-language media company, in 1997 when the stock was at $9, knowing there was a growing Latino population in the United States with increasing purchasing power, and sold that stock in 2001 at $50—for a profit of $123,000—when I saw that the game had changed and many English-language television channels were now available in Spanish. I saw that Commerce Bank in New York City was unique for being open on Sundays. It was so convenient, in fact, that I started banking there myself. Sure enough, over time more and more branches opened, and many of them stayed open until midnight. I bought the stock at $25.50 in July 2004, and sold in May 2006 at $40 because of concerns about rising interest rates and the corresponding potential economic and housing market decline. I made a profit of more than 58 percent.

You also should know that we all make mistakes, and the key is to learn from them. Personally, one of the biggest mistakes I've made is to fall in love with a stock that had made me money in the past. It's like going back to a well that's become empty. Years ago, I did this with Merck stock. It was the darling of Wall Street for years and just seemed to be going up and up, but the trend and tide suddenly turned against pharmaceutical companies. I bought Merck stock again at $63, after it had dropped from the $90s, and held on. I watched it go down to the $20s, then back up to the $50s. I've seen companies go from high-flying down to zero, so anything was possible. But I let my emotions get the best of me and neglected to be vigilant about this one. It can happen to anyone. The lesson I learned from this is to never think you're so smart or to try to catch a falling knife. When we start making a little bit of money, it's easy to get cocky. But the stock market can humble even the best of Wall Street pros, so beware.

The more you employ the trend tips I'll present, the smarter investments you will make. You will see that you can use these tips in a variety of ways. You don't need to follow one tip over another, and often you will use one tip in conjunction with another.

Getting wealthy is not something reserved for the elite or the Wall Street pros in our society. It's all about keeping your eyes and your mind open, asking questions, and developing your ability to see the patterns that create opportunities for wealth.

TREND TIP 1

Play the Six Degrees of Making Bacon

The Ripple Effect of Trends

Most people are familiar with the party game Six Degrees of Kevin Bacon: "I'm friends with Sally who has a cousin who designs sets for a director who works with Kevin Bacon." The point of the game is to link any person to Kevin Bacon through six steps or less, and it illustrates the larger "Six Degrees of Separation" theory that every person in the world is only six contacts away from knowing every other person in the world.

I have made millions by making a different set of connections and connecting the dots to an overlooked pot of gold. One of my most valuable techniques for picking stocks is to look for the "unlikely suspects." These are the companies that thrive as a supplier or the ancillary beneficiary of a trend, societal change, or economic or political driver.

While social scientists have studied how we as people are interconnected, little research has been dedicated to the significance of the relationship chain in financial trends. Economists have drawn up complicated equations for many economic models, but how an obvious trend causes other trends is relatively uncharted territory for even the professional investor. As a result, *mapping out causal connections in trends might be one of the best kept secrets to identifying and profiting from these trends.* The party game's goal is getting to Kevin Bacon in six steps. In financial trend spotting, finding a service or product that's separated—whether by two, three, or six steps—from a clear trend can lead to a great investment. For that matter, identifying a company even farther separated, whether 10, 15, or 20 degrees, can sometimes be profitable.

The best part is that it isn't rocket science.

Take the case of corn ethanol. With the rapidly growing interest in ethanol as a more environmentally friendly substitute for gasoline in the last few years, corn prices have skyrocketed. Many investors have jumped to make money off this trend. By now, the prices of corn have already jumped, leaving less potential to profit off the trend. Rather than trying to get in on something that has already become highly valued, you can make better money by applying the

Six Degrees of Making Bacon principle, and investing in more affordable options that will benefit from the newfound popularity of corn. While everyone and their brother will be investing in the trend itself, you'll be surprised how many people don't think to invest beyond the trend.

If demand for corn has risen dramatically, farmers are going to be trying to meet that demand. What products or services do they need in order to increase production of corn? For one, they're going to be buying new tractors and other farming equipment, as well as more pesticides and fertilizer. So you might want to look at companies like AGCO Corporation or John Deere, which make tractors, combines, sprayers, and other equipment. Or check out companies like Monsanto, which produces Roundup, a pesticide often used on corn and soybeans (another source of biofuels). Syngenta is another example: among other things, they develop high-performing seeds, including corn seed, and are creating a hybrid corn specifically for improved biofuel. Then there are middlemen like Archer Daniels Midland, which stores, transports, and processes agricultural products, as well as train manufacturers like American Railcar, which makes and services trains used to carry agricultural products. The list could go on and on.

Drawing Connections

I find the easiest way to play the Six Degrees game is to draw diagrams. It's fun to uncover how an obvious trend has a ripple effect. You can usually find products, services, and companies worldwide in every direction that are positively affected by a trend.

Don't just think in a linear way. The ripple effects of just one trend can take you numerous steps in many different directions. In order to play the Six Degrees of Making Bacon, all you need is a bit of creativity.

Let's look at an example. Beginning in January 2001, interest rates started to drop. When the Federal Reserve Board lowers the federal funds rate, the prime rate follows the trend downward, as do mortgage rates. The trend of falling interest rates invariably lights a fire under the housing market. When mortgage interest rates are low, people can afford to buy houses that they couldn't buy when the interest rates were higher.

So we draw our first set of connections:

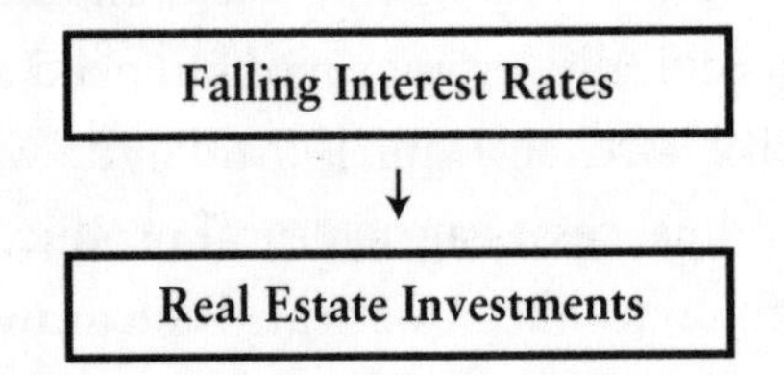

If you bet on housing to be a big market as we headed into the twenty-first century, you were right. The value of residential real estate in the United States rose by about ten trillion dollars from 2000 to 2005, with the average home costing over 60 percent more than it had at the end of 1999. So just one degree away from the trend of falling interest rates, you would have found a great way to profit. But now take it several steps farther. Cheap mortgages mean more people will take a mortgage, which means there will be a spurt in the new-home market. Home builders are ready to rock when those rates fall.

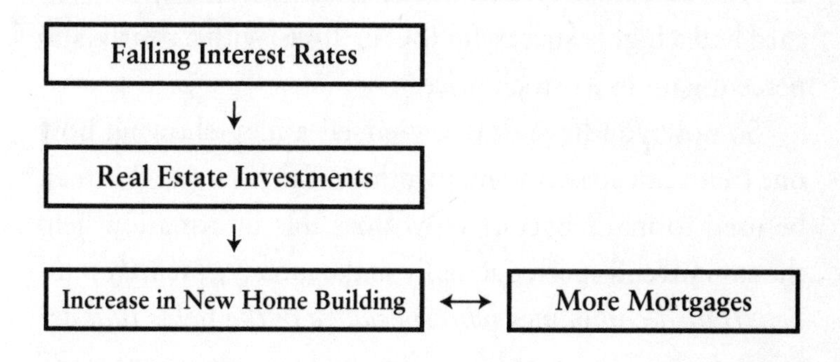

Now take it farther still. When home building is on the rise, what other products and services are positively affected? Building materials, construction crews, home design companies, for starters. When mortgage companies do well, who else does well? Sub-prime lenders, secondary mortgage buyers, and banks, among others.

Once you start the game it's hard to stop. In our country of hungry consumerism, low interest rates also tempt people to stop saving altogether. In fact, they start to borrow at low interest rates and to "cash-out refinance" so they can buy goods they've always wanted (but really can't afford)—a new SUV, a cruise, a Jacuzzi on the back deck, expensive shoes. How do they do most of their borrowing? In the form of credit cards. This is good news for the credit companies as well as the companies servicing the credit companies—including not just credit card equipment makers but credit counselors and the debt collection companies.

It is no coincidence that the stock of American Express grew steadily in these five years, almost doubling in price, and I recommended its stock consistently on Fox News from 2001 to 2003. It's also no coincidence that Mastercard had a highly successful IPO in 2006, with a nearly 300 percent gain in its stock price.

So now you have drawn yourself a map showing how one trend can spawn so many others. But how can this map be used to make bacon? How does this information help the savvy trend spotter actually make money? *Identify publicly traded companies who specialize in the fields that are some degrees separated from an obvious trend source, and consider investing in these companies.*

For example, on my AOL blog, I recommended West Corporation in November 2005, back when it was trading just below $40.89. This company collects receivables for other corporations. Knowing that America's debt was getting out of hand, after being spurred on by the rise in home-equity loans, I believed West Corp.'s collection services would be in increasing demand. Sure enough, in late 2006, West Corp. was bought by Quadrangle, and each investor received $48.75 per share. Someone who had bought $2,700 in West Corp. stock back in November 2005 would have sold at $3,219—for a gain of $519, or nearly 20 percent. Not a bad return for a year!

Take another example. During the housing boom, I invested in New Century Financial, which offers sub-prime residential loans. Sub-prime mortgages are high-risk. They

Trend Tip 1: Play the Six Degrees of Making Bacon

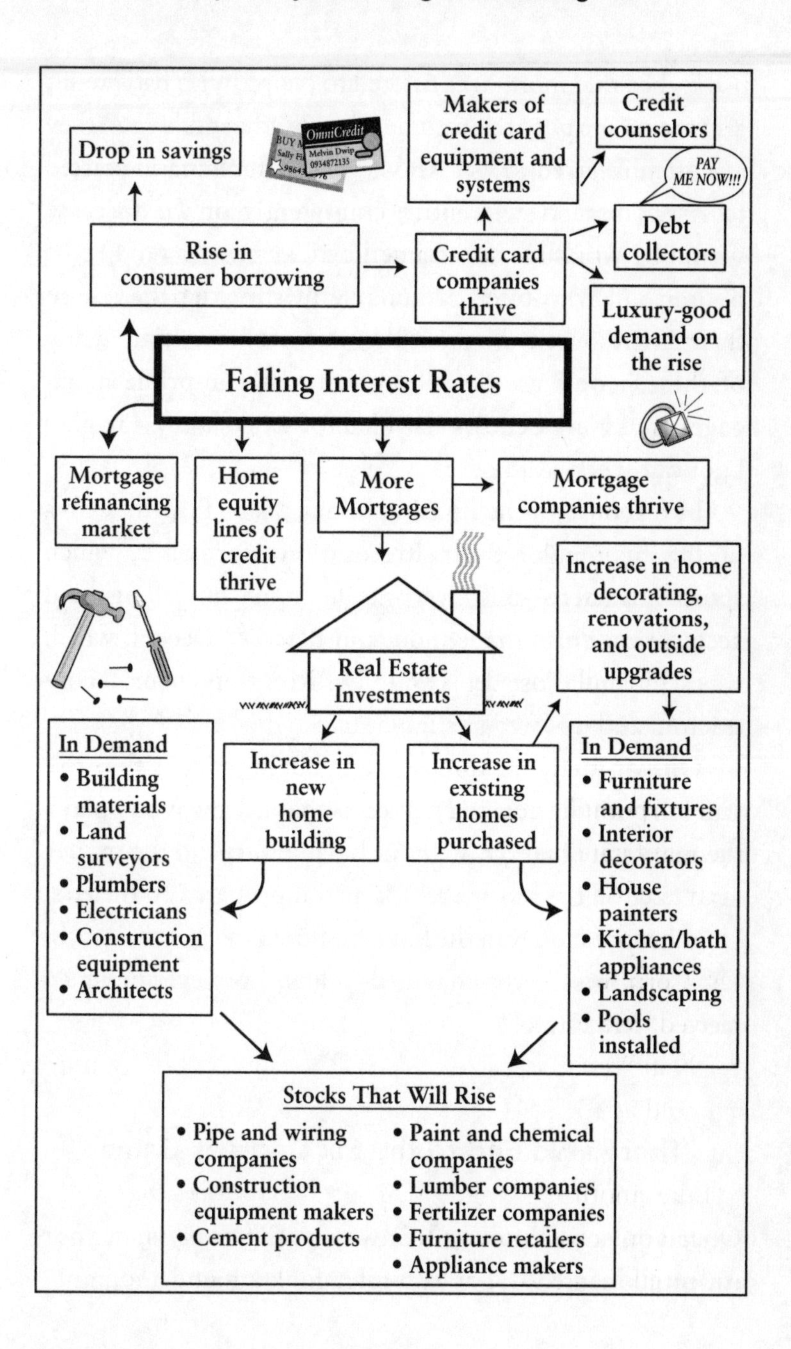

are higher-rate mortgages offered to people with bad credit, and the majority of them come with an adjustable rate (they are often referred to as "ARMs"). As interest rates started to rise, I sold New Century, knowing that the increase would be worst for sub-prime borrowers, who tend to be poorer and who often are unable to shoulder the rise in their ARM. Sure enough, at the time of this writing, many of these people are defaulting on their sub-prime mortgages, and New Century has filed for bankruptcy. I'm glad I got out when I did.

In response to the housing boom, I also bought shares of the high-end retailer Restoration Hardware, which sports attractive—and overpriced—home furnishings and accessories. I also made money in Black & Decker, which was selling all those drills and saws to entrepreneurial contractors and do-it-yourselfers.

One of the great things about buying stocks that rise and fall with the housing market is that it's a way to "play" the real estate market, without having to spend the money (and take on the mortgage) for actual property. In the end, I made more money in the housing-boom market than most "house flippers" ever imagined—all without ever buying a piece of real estate!

There's No End to the Six Degrees Game

Once you start thinking this way, you'll easily spin your own webs of trends. For example, think about demographics. The aging of Baby Boomers means more future health care needs, such as hospitalization, pharmaceuticals, artificial joints, and even ambulance transport. I own stock in Rural/Metro, a small ambulance company based in Arizona—a place full of senior citizens. In time, I am sure that stock will double. I also recommended Sunrise Senior Living in early 2006, right after a delayed earnings announcement caused its stock price to dip. I predicted it would drop from $35 to $25 but then climb back up to $45. Since then, it dropped to nearly $26, but has already come back above $40. Why? Because it is a smart company offering specialized assisted-living services to seniors. With the aging of the U.S. population, I believe Sunrise is destined for decades of strong growth.

Similarly, Cantel Medical produces sterilization and sanitization systems as well as other medical supplies for hospitals, dentists, and doctors. With these products likely to be in greater demand owing to an aging population, it's no surprise that Cantel's price rose nearly 25 percent in the six months after I picked it. Then there's Bio-Reference Lab, which offers clinical laboratory testing services in the Greater New York area. I picked this stock in April 2006, after its price had quadrupled over the previous five years. Despite that growth, I predicted there was still room for more upside for this highly profitable company. Within eight months, the stock price was up another 50 percent.

You may have missed the housing boom or gotten in late on the baby boomer trend, but you can take comfort in the fact that we are about to embark on one of the biggest trends of the past fifty years. This trend encompasses transportation, agriculture, chemicals, manufacturing, biotechnology, and even real estate. I'm referring to the Green Revolution—the developments that will take place in clean technology, alternative energy, and environmental enhancements and remediation. You don't have to make your money by investing directly in an ethanol plant or in a solar power company. You can invest in John Deere, for example, which will be needed to produce more tractors to help harvest the preferred crop used for biofuel—whatever crop it ultimately turns out to be. Better yet, as more crops are used for fuel instead of feed, the cost of beef and chicken will likely rise and consumers may turn more to other forms of protein, such as fish. So why not look for companies specializing in fish products?

The Green Revolution isn't the only trend on the horizon. The great part about this game is that it is a tool for constantly identifying new opportunities.

Not Every Company Connected to a Trend Is a Winner

You can play this game to great profit, provided the connections you make in linking one category to another are sound and you select companies in the best positions to thrive from the trend. Don't assume that just because, say, nails are needed for the home-building boom, Nails and

Screws, Inc. necessarily will prove to be a good investment. Don't throw your money into every company involved in any of the six (or more) degrees separated from a trend. Just because the trend is a winner doesn't mean a particular company is capable of or positioned for taking advantage of that trend.

There are two crucial things to keep in mind when following all the trend tips I'll introduce for deciding whether a company you think will be positively affected by a trend is worth pouring your money into:

First, whenever possible, *invest in a company you know and like.* If you are constantly impressed when you visit a Lowe's, then it's likely that others feel the same way. On the other hand, if you find yourself frustrated and dissatisfied when you visit a Home Depot, then I doubt that you are alone. In early 2006, I wrote a scathing AOL blog entry about my experience shopping in a Home Depot, where I could never find anyone to help me with what I was looking for. Most people I know had the same experience. I predicted this would eventually hurt the company, and I was right. Several months later, the stock had dipped nearly 23 percent. To be sure, Home Depot was also hurt by the softening housing market, but its rival Lowe's, which was hurt by the housing market as well, dropped less and made up more ground faster. In my blog pick, I praised Lowe's customer service, and I'm certain that quality of service has had much to do with Lowe's better results.

Next, *study the company financials,* which you can find painlessly on the internet—both in the company's own reports to investors and on many reliable financial sites. Remember what I said about always doing your homework. It is important that you educate yourself about how to read a balance sheet and an income statement. It is also important to go to the source. Look directly at the company's balance sheet, which can be found in its annual report to investors and also on the SEC's sec.gov website (in the form of the annual 10-K and the quarterly 10-Q filings). There are many good books and online sites that can educate you in the basics of investing and analyzing the strength of a company. In the appendixes you'll find more information to help you understand the specifics of this analysis.

The key metrics that I examine when assessing a company are the company's financial fundamentals, profitability, rate of growth, stock value, and management. Here's a quick overview of rules of thumb to follow.

Basics of Assessing the Strength of a Company

1. *Financial fundamentals*: A company must have solid fundamentals. To assess these, you can easily calculate these ratios:
   a. *Quick ratio:* This figure is called the "quick ratio" because it gives you a quick snapshot of the company's solidness. It measures the liquidity of a company—its ability to make good on its obligations. Take the current assets of the company, subtract from them the inventories, and divide this

figure by the current liabilities. And if you don't feel like doing math, many reliable financial sites will have calculated the number for you (see Appendix A). *The higher this number in comparison with other companies in its field, the more financially sound the company.*

b. *Debt/equity ratio:* Heavy debt is a bad sign. By dividing the debt of a company by its equity, you can calculate this ratio. The lower this figure, the better. If the number is nearing 40–50 percent, you should take a very careful look at why, particularly if the company has a low quick ratio, indicating that it could have potential problems paying off debt in the near future.

   Companies with that high level of debt traditionally will be using a large portion of their annual earnings to pay interest and principal on that debt, rather than using it to pay dividends or to invest in future growth, both of which would help you as an investor.

2. *Profitability*: The *profit margin* is the gross profit (or the profit once you've subtracted out the cost of the goods) divided by the total revenue, and it indicates the efficiency and profitability of a business. The higher this number, the better. Investors like to find companies that continue to increase their profit margins over the years, signaling that they are staying competitive while remaining profitable. Again, compare the profit margins of a company with those of competitors in its industry to

gain insight into the strength of the company relative to other companies in the same business. (Average profit margins of companies in different industries are all over the place: from 20–25 percent in certain types of manufacturing to well over 70 percent in some service businesses.)

3. *Growth*: A company may be debt-free, but unless it has strong growth potential, your investment won't be likely to have strong growth potential, either. One indicator of a company's growth potential is its historical growth rate. Look at the *growth rate* figures to see if there has been fairly consistent growth (in profits and/or revenues, depending on the industry) over the last year, five years, and ten years, and compare the figures with those of other companies in its industry. (See Appendix A for where to find these growth rates.)

   An anomalous short-term burst of growth yesterday means little today. Steady upward growth, however, indicates it will likely continue into the future, if everything else about the company checks out. Good smaller companies (those with less revenue) should generally have higher growth rates than larger companies (those with more revenue).

4. *Value:* Check out the company's *price-to-earnings ratio* (known as the *P/E ratio*), which is the price per share divided by the earning per share, and compare it with that of others in the same business to determine if the company is "overvalued." In the simplest sense, the P/E ratio tells you how much you need to pay to own $1 of

the company earnings. A high price-to-earnings ratio thus might indicate that investors think the company is poised to grow. However, compare it with other companies in the same industry. If Nails and Screws, Inc. has a P/E ratio of 30, whereas its competitors have P/Es of 15, it may be that Nails and Screws, Inc. is overvalued. But refer back to the growth rate before deciding to punt it. Perhaps Nails and Screws, Inc. has comparable profit margins, but enjoys a much higher growth rate than its competitors, warranting its higher P/E ratio.

Remember the principle to buy low, sell high. You are looking for the gems: undervalued, solid companies that are about to benefit from a trend. A low P/E in the Six Degrees of Making Bacon game is a good sign that you could really profit from the investment, and if the growth rate is strong as well, then you have likely found a good target.

5. *Management*: Make sure the company has effective and experienced management in place. You can find the professional backgrounds of top executives on the company's website. Another positive sign is when management holds significant amounts of stock in the company—several times their base pay. (This information is available on sites like Yahoo! Finance and MSN Money.) It indicates that the leaders are personally vested to make the company work in the long term; since they aren't just working for a paycheck, they actually own part of it. It's even more encouraging when

they're buying additional shares with their own money. Take a look at the pay structure. Are executives reasonably compensated in comparison with other heads in their fields? Are the senior executives overcompensated compared with their peers? And look, too, at the company's dividend policies, found in their annual reports. A good leader is thinking about how to spend, invest, or distribute company profits fairly to his or her shareholders. Ask whether the company management is forward thinking, preparing to capitalize on the trend you've identified as coming their way. Is Nails and Screws, Inc. in a good place to beat competing nail manufacturers? Are they putting money toward research and development of new and improved nails? Are they creatively and effectively marketing their screws? You can get a sense of a management team's thinking on these issues from the CEO's annual letter to shareholders in the company's annual report and from the presentations to investors (usually in the "investor relations" section of a company's website).

One other key tip is to always take a look at the pending-litigation section of the SEC documents. Although every company is at one time or another the subject of some lawsuit—usually frivolous—I have also found insights into pending issues that will become important with time.

One critical item to remember in this analysis is to compare companies in the same line of business. Otherwise, the actual ratio, margin, rate, or multiple doesn't have much meaning. After all, Google, for example, will (and should) have very different profit margins from, say, Coca-Cola. But it matters a lot more how Coca-Cola performs relative to its peers, like Pepsico, when evaluating how well an investment in that company's stock can ride the wave of a trend. Let's say you conclude that the beverage industry is poised for growth. After doing some homework, you find that the growth rate for Coca-Cola is higher than that of the beverage industry overall. You know then that Coca-Cola's growth isn't only from capitalizing on the growth trend in the beverage market, but that the incremental growth means it's actually doing a *better* job of capitalizing on that trend than its competitors (perhaps even taking business away from them). So if you want to take advantage of the beverage industry growth trend in this example, you'd probably be better off investing in Coca-Cola over its competitors.

Okay, so let's take a look at how you could have played the Six Degrees game, following these rules of thumb, at the start of the housing boom. Let's say you did some shopping around home improvement stores in the public market space. You checked out the fundamentals of Lowe's home improvement stores and they seemed solid. You'd been to Home Depot and had concerns about their customer service that worried you about the company's long-term potential. Then you discovered that the only other real competitors of Lowe's were Sherwin-Williams, Ace Hardware, and TrueValue (and the latter two are privately held and therefore not traded as stocks on any exchange). In any case, the sales generated by Home Depot and Lowe's dwarfed those of the other three (even combined), so it was down to a two-horse race. Toward the end of February 2001, you picked up 100 shares of Lowe's at $14.25. In 2004, when interest rates were again on the rise, you decided that the home improvement market might begin to suffer, so three years after your stock purchase, toward the end of February 2004 you sold the 100 shares at $29.00 per share. In three years, your $1,425 investment became $2,900. That's a home run where you finished your jog around the bases without breaking a sweat.

How to Know When a Trend Is Peaking

It's well and good to identify a trend and to ride it, but unless you jump on and off at the right times, the exercise will be pointless, and you can lose money. You need to be careful about your timing, about evaluating where you are on the trend curve. You have to know whether the trend is still growing or whether you're too late. This is the "vigilance" part of being patient and vigilant. New Century Financial is a perfect example of that. Investors who didn't pay attention to the changing landscape and held onto New Century lost quite a bit of money. Don't wait for the brokers and analysts to warn you. Keep your eyes open and remember that gravity and momentum bring us down faster than we rise. The last thing you want is to invest on the slippery slope of the other side of the trend's peak.

But how do you know when a trend is nearing its peak? There is no hard and fast rule of thumb, but looking at examples of similar trends in stock market history will help. Let's take the housing market again. Take a look below at how, as interest rates fell in the last boom, various sectors benefited—-from home builders like KB Home, to home improvement retailers like Lowe's, to mortgage providers like New Century.

Interest rates reached lows in 2002 and 2003 and then began to rise. New Century stock started to fall before 2005, while Lowe's continued to ride generally upward through 2006, as did KB Home. No question, other factors impacted these specific companies, and you as an investor will benefit from looking at many charts from similar companies in the home building sector to get a feel for this, but it gives a general sense of trend curves.

In making the timing decision, it's fine not to worry if you jump off a bit early or a bit late. You might not make every single cent that you could have made, but you will still have profited, which is the name of the trend-riding game. And sometimes a stock will take a temporary dive down or a jag up, so don't assume that any down tick is the trigger to sell.

Keep your eye closely on your investments, as there are so many developments that can adversely or positively help a company (sometimes, things that have nothing to do with trends—like lawsuits). Check your portfolio weekly to make sure the stock isn't slipping downward, and do your own reality check on the company to make sure it still is the strong, trend-riding company that you thought it was when you bought it. I also set "alerts" through websites like Google, Yahoo!, MarketWatch, MSN Money, and broker sites so that when a company is in the news, I receive an email. Another great way to get continual updates is to sign up with companies themselves to receive their press releases.

Because the Six Degrees game is so enjoyable, it's also easy to go too far. That's why it's essential to follow some basic guidelines in using it as a trend tool:

Don't ignore human nature. Humans don't change easily, so be careful in the kinds of connections you make. For instance, you might look at the hole in the ozone layer, which has led to an increased incidence of skin cancer and the growing use of sunscreen. Naturally, you might think, the popularity of tanning booths would decline, following this trend. But people love being tan, and vanity often wins out over common sense. Men and women are still soaking up the rays, and tanning booths are thriving. Trend Tip 3 delves more deeply into the role of human nature in determining trends.

Don't force connections. Don't assume too much or push a connection too far. Easy does it with this type of investing method. Be smart in connecting the dots, and do your research. Take nuclear power, which could be an alternative energy source as we try to limit greenhouse gases. You might think Toshiba, which owns Westinghouse, which is building nuclear energy facilities in China, would be a good bet. But there are still many concerns about nuclear waste, and it will take a long time before the world makes a significant move to nuclear power. Make sure you think things through and do your homework before jumping to invest.

Don't jump on every wagon. Just because a company is in an industry that has potential to benefit from a trend doesn't mean that the company will be a winning investment. If the company's financials, management, or other fundamentals aren't strong, it will likely not succeed, despite the positive environment in which it competes. Of course, in the very short run, even trendy companies that aren't well equipped for the future enjoy the wind beneath their wings, but they ultimately crash or at least underperform.

Nothing is written in stone. While trends are great indicators of a company's potential, external factors can arise that add kinks into the equation. The genius CEO might get hit by a bus, an act of God might ruin the crops, or a war might keep people from leaving home. Or a new company or technology might enter the scene and render everyone else obsolete. As with all risks, assess them based on sound information. This is exactly why I stressed diversifying your portfolio, so that you spread your risks around a number of companies and sectors. Even if an unforeseeable factor hurts one of your trends or stocks, being diversified across different trends and stocks should allow you to come out ahead in the long run.

When telling yourself not to sweat too much over missed opportunities, remember that investing is like driving. You need to always be looking forward instead of in the rearview mirror. Save looking back for reflecting and learning, not for regretting.

TREND TIP 2

Think Like a Detective

Detective Work Pays When It Comes to Trends

Nancy Drew, famous girl detective of Carolyn Keene's evergreen series, didn't have any training to be a private eye. She was simply observant and knew how to put two and two together. Whether a clue was a seemingly innocuous copy of a newspaper or a bracelet with a family crest, she'd spot it—she always kept her eyes peeled for signs that something was afoot. And at the end of the day, she would solve her case. Always.

Whenever someone asks me how to discover trends

before everyone else, I say, *Be a Nancy Drew.* As you go about your life and business, wear your detective hat at all times. (If you don't like Nancy, feel free to consider yourself an Encyclopedia Brown or Sherlock Holmes.) Some of the best research isn't done by studying the financials on Morningstar, but by being acutely aware of what's going on around you. You don't need to be a brilliant theorist or business school graduate. You don't need to understand the detailed financial figures in a company's tax reports in order to figure out where and when the next trend will be heading.

Go shopping—in discount warehouses and in high-end specialty boutiques—and observe the foot traffic in the stores. Who is buying what computers? Who is buying shoes, and from where? Ask the salesperson what's selling. When you visit the doctor, ask what he or she is prescribing most often. At a baseball game, look around you. Are there certain well-placed ads that catch your eye? When you're grocery shopping, do you notice that certain brand products are represented in every cart in the checkout line? At the movies, pay attention to which products are getting special placement. At a dinner party, keep your ears open for comments about products. On the highway, pay attention to the models of cars people are driving (but do keep your eye on the road!). You never know where you're going to get a great lead.

I never turn my detective mind off. This way of doing research doesn't feel like a chore; on the contrary, it's great fun. When the babysitter came over the other day to take my daughter to the park, she and I spoke in Spanish about how much she loved a new food product being sold in all the grocery stores. Later, I checked it out and realized that it was a new company serving the growing Hispanic market in a very savvy way. I flagged it as a company to keep my eye on. The other day, a friend told me about a new home health care service in which she had enrolled her aging father. I wrote it into my Black-Berry, where I keep lots of notes of this kind to myself. I return to these notes regularly, and do the research on the new companies I've identified to see if they are worth investing in, or perhaps to keep an eye on for down the road.

I could give you innumerable examples of how keeping my eyes peeled in everyday life has helped me spot trends and ride them before others. But I'll stick to just a few examples for now. You'd be surprised how easy it is.

As I've said before: I travel all the time. It is part of my business. Rather than zoning out, waiting to get from point A to point B, I use travel as great opportunity to spy trends. A few years back, I couldn't help but notice that the planes I was flying on always seemed to be Embraer jets. I knew this had to be for a good reason. When I did my research, I learned that Embraer is a strong Brazilian company that has become one of the largest aerospace manufacturers in the world. They make aircraft for commercial airlines and the military, and they're particularly known for their smaller planes, which are good for the regional routes that are being traveled more and more in recent years. These routes aren't traveled enough to require larger planes, and the smaller jets that Embraer makes allow airliners to make higher profits by using less fuel. At the time I bought this stock, in 2003, it was trading at $15. At the time of writing this book, it is around $48.

As you do your detective work, make sure to keep these factors in mind:

Keep an Open Mind

Just because you've always done something a certain way doesn't mean times don't change. Don't disregard out of hand things you find foolish or frivolous simply because you would not be interested in them, if many others are fascinated by them. Take the video game craze. The last video game I think I played was Ms. Pac-Man in the early 1980s. These games make me dizzy, and I can't stand how they eat into my time (no pun intended). But I'd be a fool not to notice the Xbox and PlayStation, and now Wii, culture booming around me. The video game industry has generated more than $7 billion in revenues each year since 2002, and it shows no signs of slowing down. Whether or not you like these games, there's money to be made from investing in the manufacturers of game systems.

It's not just to be made in those large, well-known companies that manufacture the systems, like Microsoft (Xbox) or Sony (PlayStation) either. While watching the popular movie *Swingers* in 1996, you might have noticed that Vince

Vaughn and the rest of those "typical guys" were really into a hockey video game. You might then have put two and two together and realized that this is the same game your younger brother or your nephew was always playing with his friends. You might then have decided to check out whether this game was making a lot of money for the company that designed it. Pursuing your lead like a good detective, you'd have found that the game was made by an undervalued company called Electronic Arts, and that it was enormously popular among young men from college age through their twenties. How would you know it was undervalued? You would have checked out their financials, including comparing their price-to-earnings ratio with those of competitors like Activision and Take-Two Interactive, two other leading interactive entertainment software publishers. Electronic Arts had a comparatively low P/E ratio, while it had signs of terrific growth moving forward, coupled with strong management and product lines. If you'd then, in 1996, invested in the company, you could have bought it at around $6; since then, the stock has climbed as high as $70 and spent much of its time around $50. That's a serious profit.

Your Teenager May Know More than You

Spend, spend, spend: there seems to be no end to the cost of having children. While you may find yourself paying through the nose for things for your children—from the designer clothes they are begging to buy, to the schoolbooks they need for studies, to the toys they choose to play with—the truth is, if you are carefully attuned to their habits, they can help you make back some of the money you have to spend on them. Who says kids don't know anything?

Kids tend to be much more tuned into the tiny changes in products and services that may turn into trends. Every day at school, they are exposed to what amounts to a minimarket of other kids all displaying things that are hot and things that they love. This is why many companies spend a good deal on focus groups trying to pick the brains of children.

For a perfect example: my friend's daughter tipped her off to the MySpace.com phenomenon well before many investors discovered this online social networking community. If only she had shared the tip with me! I could have bought shares in Intermix, the company that owned MySpace, back in March 2004 when the stock price was still below $3. If I'd bought then and held the stock until October 2005, when Rupert Murdoch's News Corp. bought Intermix to get MySpace.com, I'd have received $12 a share. There were lots of incentives for me to dump my shares in the meantime, as there was an investigation of Intermix by the New York State Attorney General. (Intermix ultimately paid $7.5 million to settle the case.) In the end, my $1,500 investment in March 2004 would have made me a cool $4,500 in about a year and a half.

Listen to Your Neighbors

You may not like their taste in decorating or their barking dog, but as a savvy detective, you can learn surprising amounts from those people around you but not close to you. Talk to everyone you can—not just the neighbors but your plumber, your electrician, the guy bagging your groceries, your lawyer, and your mom. Ask questions. Find out what *they* think is hot, exciting, novel, useful. In short, find out how they are spending their money.

Back in 2003, a friend who sadly was battling multiple sclerosis called me, excited about a new injectable drug that would help her manage her illness. I checked out the drug online and did some research. It was being manufactured by Teva Pharmaceutical Industries Ltd. (TEVA). This is an Israeli generic-pharmaceuticals company. At the time, it was at $17 a share, and it had solid financials and good management, so I snapped some up. Today, at the time of writing this book, it is up to $35. And during 2006, it had gotten as high as $46.

I never leave home without my detective magnifying glass. In August 2003, for example, I went to visit my best friend's parents in Odessa, Texas. I wasn't planning on learning anything—just going to relax with people I love. My friend's father is a salesman for Weatherford International Ltd. (WFT), which provides equipment and services for oil well drilling. Weatherford helps oil and natural gas companies determine where to drill, and offers equipment to access the oil and gas as well as pipelines to transport it. We went with my friend's father to visit his clients. They all were buying machinery and equipment. But the problem, I was told, was that there wasn't enough equipment and labor to fulfill all the demand for oil.

That was all I needed to know. It was clear that oil and gas companies were going to need to increase their production, and that a company that could help them accomplish this was going to make lots of money in the coming years. When I returned home from the trip and did some more research on Weatherford and its financials, I was all the more convinced. I bought WFT at $18, and I sold in the summer of 2006 for $50.

Patterns and Connections

Like a good PI, connect the dots. If your daughter is listening to an iPod and your hairdresser and your cousin in Minnesota are also listening to iPods, that should tell you something. *Look for widespread trends.* If you see the same trend emerging in distant parts of the country, there's a great chance it's for real. A friend of mine is a pilot for a major airline. In the summer of 2004 she started complaining about how children were bringing these stuffed animals in boxes onto the plane and taking up seat space. I thought to myself, How odd. A stuffed animal that is so popular that a pilot is noticing them on the planes!

I inquired some more. Turns out, my pilot friend was

referring to the signature Build-A-Bear boxes. I looked up the company online and saw the amazing potential in this retail-tainment concept, in which parents can take their young children to build and customize their own bears. But being wowed by an online description is nothing like seeing it with one's own eyes. I went to my local mall and noticed the line snaking out the Build-A-Bear door. Research into the company's S-1 filing (which is the financial and business description form all companies must file with the SEC before a public stock offering) confirmed the store's popularity. Between 2001 and 2004, the company more than doubled its number of stores from 71 to 150, and its revenues doubled from $106 million to $213 million, all while more than quadrupling net income from $1.9 million to $8 million.

So as soon as it went public in October 2004, I bought 1,000 shares at $25 a share. Within a couple months it was at $35; I was tempted to sell, thinking it had become overvalued by investors, but I didn't want to take the tax hit on such a quick transaction. (Holding a stock for more than a year allows you to treat the sales as long-term capital gains: taxed at 15 percent versus your normal income tax rate.) So I held it, and watched the stock drop to $30—and then to $20 by the summer of 2005. It seemed many investors had decided this was a fad and were selling as soon as the stock started dropping, but I was still seeing the Build-A-Bear stores packed whenever I went to the mall, so I refused to take a loss. Sure enough, the stock began climbing again, and as soon as it got up above $30 in late 2005, I sold my shares (at around $31) for a gain of about $6,000, or about 24 percent, and a much smaller tax hit than I'd have incurred if I'd sold it in the summer of 2005.

Go Where the People Go

The previous example feeds directly into this helpful hint. Follow the crowd, whether it's the line snaking around the mall leading to Build-A-Bear or the one at the register at Sephora. Crowds tell you more than the financial pages can ever predict. When you're hungry, and you walk into a new Mexican chain restaurant in Washington, D.C., and find it packed with people, and the same thing happens in a few more cities, or friends in other cities mention the chain, you should make note that people really seem to be liking Chipotle. That's what happened to me in early 2006. So I looked up the company, liked how its financials compared with those of industry peers, bought the stock around $45, and have watched it climb to $80. I've made a nice return on it, and I enjoy the food a little more each time I go.

I have also made money by paying attention to the growing lines in the dressing rooms of some of my favorite stores. I've always been a huge fan of TJ Maxx and Marshalls, and I'm not afraid to admit they're my favorite places to shop. It's not just the satisfaction of finding nice clothes that look great and cost half, or even a third, of what I'd pay in a department store (forget about a boutique). It's not even the secret pleasure I get when my fancier friends or colleagues ask me if I got my fabulous outfit at some chic retailer. For me, shopping at TJ Maxx is like treasure hunting—it's a game, and I thoroughly enjoy it even when I don't find anything to buy. Much of the fun is in the search.

I'd been shopping at these stores for years when I noticed it was getting harder to find things, and the lines were much longer at the dressing room and at the cash register. This was back in 2000, when the economy was starting to slow down. The stock markets were declining even as the average American's share of stock holdings was nearing an all-time high. Large corporations were in cost-cutting mode, which threatened to leave many workers unemployed. This, after a few years of dot-com excess, left many consumers with high levels of personal debt. As I waited in line to check out at TJ Maxx one day, I realized the crowds were there for a special reason: with the economic future less certain, people were trying to cut costs where they could, and were going to the discount stores in much larger numbers.

I went home that afternoon, did some research on the TJ Maxx financials, and bought shares in TJX, the ownership company, when the price was still below $10. Since then it has risen steadily, and my investment has nearly tripled as the stock price has climbed toward $30. It's been a bit more volatile than I would have liked, as the companies that sell excess merchandise are managing their inventories better, and thus there are fewer overruns for TJ Maxx to offer, but I'm continuing to hold it. I believe the desire for cheap, quality clothing is a long-term trend, though of course, as with all the stocks in my portfolio, I'll keep monitoring the situation closely.

All Eyes on the Experts

Read what the analysts have to say and weigh their assessments against what you are observing. This helpful tip may seem counter to the advice I often dish out. You'll hear me say again and again that you can learn more by keeping an open mind and not believing everything that is being broadcast through the media. After all, you're not the only one, by a long shot, who is tuning into the experts' opinions, so it's hard to use their advice to ride a trend before others are surfing it. But I still believe in paying attention to what they're saying. The key is to use their words as clues and not to just uncritically follow their advice.

For one thing, as I discussed earlier, some trends aren't going away, and they're worth getting in on even if not right at the beginning of the opportunity. Also, you can always use a tip from the experts to play the Six Degrees of Making Bacon. At the time of this writing, analysts are predicting that with cell phones offering more and more features—Mp3 player, banking capabilities, even multiplayer video games—the future of telecom is extremely bright. But maybe you feel you've already missed out on companies like Verizon or Nokia. Rather than giving up, look into the bandwidth issues that are likely to arise as telephones send and receive more and more information. For example, find a company that provides infrastructure for wireless and cellular coverage, do your research, and if it looks promising, you might want to take a chance on it.

Even more helpful than the talking head–type experts are the experts in the field. Look at what the experts in the trenches are doing. By this, I mean the big, successful venture capitalists and the private equity hotshots. There is to my mind no better analysis resource than these folks. They are the smartest of the smart, and I like to say, "Go where the smart money goes." In other words, where are the world's top venture capital firms pouring their money? Articles in financial magazines and in *Fortune* or *The Wall Street Journal* will sometimes address this issue. Do web searches as well, such as for "venture capital investments" on Google News. Pay attention. Read blogs. Also keep an eye on the local papers from places on the West Coast like Silicon Valley, where many VC firms are based. I read the *San Jose Mercury News* and *The Seattle Times* for this reason. Those publications are usually well tuned in to the tech- and VC-related business gossip, and you can quickly get a clear picture of which trends VCs are investing in.

For an example of watching where the VC money is going, in early 2007 you might have read that Accel Partners, Sequoia Capital, and Kleiner Perkins Caufield & Byers, to name a few of the high-level venture capital firms, were focusing investment dollars on start-up companies specializing in person-to-person communication and interacting over the web—activities like video and photo sharing. Their strategies had paid off in the past. Take Sequoia's investment in YouTube.com. When in October 2006, Google, Inc. announced its pending $1.65 billion purchase of YouTube, Sequoia stood to make a staggering $500 million.

How could knowing about Sequoia's initial investment in YouTube help you? Well, say you were tracking a venture capital firm that you respected, like Sequoia. When they put their money into a business (and you read about it on their website or in the *San Jose Mercury News*), it can mean only one thing: they think they can make money off the company. Venture capital is high-risk but high-reward. They don't take on charity cases; in other words, when they put their money into a company, they expect results—and even better, they are often key players in driving results, helping to shape management and strategy.

But don't trust them entirely. As always, do your research, too: What does that company make or provide? How are they run? If the fundamentals look good and you feel confident in their product or service and in their lasting power, then you may want to jump in at the stage of the initial public offering.

Log On, Tune In

Venture capitalists, as smart as they are, often miss the trend, too. Bessemer Venture Partners, a long-time successful VC firm willing to poke fun at itself, has on its website an amusing "anti-portfolio" composed of companies they had a chance to invest in but passed on. Notable companies include the likes of eBay ("Stamps? Coins? Comic books? You've *got* to be kidding. No-brainer pass"), Apple, Google, and FedEx (passed on it seven different times). They missed some big ones! So where else can you go to get the latest scoops? What's going on in the internet community—in blogs, where traffic flows, and chat rooms—can tell you a ton about trends. You might not believe this, but I even turn off the spam filter on my email. Sure, I get some unsavory emails that tell me nothing, but I also get a sense of where the general pulse of the culture is headed. I read my favorite financial blogs daily. The chat rooms on the financial sites help me get a sense of the general public's perceptions. Remember this: The stock market is all about perception. Best Company USA may have an amazing product and be well run; but if it is trending out of favor in the minds of the public, for whatever reason, it will probably not be a good stock pick.

Whole Foods is a great example of this phenomenon. They're sprouting up left and right, their profits continue to rise, they always seem to be packed, and they're right in line with the public's growing interest in organic foods. For a while, the stock price reflected this, soaring from around $20 to $76 in just over four years. But at some point, a backlash started. I noticed people complaining about the prices and the lines, and the company's growth made it seem more like a big corporation than the local market it had portrayed itself as. After reaching its $76 peak in early 2006, Whole

Foods' stock started losing ground rapidly, and it nearly halved in price in the space of a single year. Yet the stores are still packed and the profits are strong and growing. What gives? It's one of those perception things, and even a well-run company like Whole Foods isn't immune.

What Would Leo Do?

If you're like me, you're not afraid to take a peek at the celebrity tabloids in the supermarket checkout line. I also admit to devouring my *People* magazine as soon as it arrives in my mailbox. While I confess that I love the gossip and pictures, I also feel fine about reading it: it can be considered financial research. Many trends are created by stars. Be pop culture savvy. Look to certain icons in our culture to set trends and anticipate them.

We all remember Beatle haircuts, don't we? These days most teenage girls dress like Britney Spears and most teenage boys look like their favorite hip-hop star. That said, be smart. When Britney Spears shaved her head in 2007, we didn't expect to see young girls throughout the country jump onboard. But when you see a pack of celebrities all embracing something, you should take particular note. A great example of this is the Toyota Prius car. After 9/11, when the world was more and more aware of the dangers of our dependence on foreign sources of oil, the stars leapt on the cause with vigor. From Larry David to Cameron Diaz to Brad Pitt, we witnessed a slew of major Hollywood players making a big deal about their fuel-efficient cars. Then, in February 2003, a PR agency asked for five Priuses to showcase at the Academy Awards. Trading in the high $40s at the time, Toyota's stock started climbing; it was around $60 at the launch of the refined Prius in the autumn of 2003, and it has climbed above $130 in the subsequent three years. It wasn't only the celebrities, of course, who drove up price—rising gas prices were also a huge factor—but the stars' early support definitely signaled a market trend.

Keeping your eyes wide open to the opportunities presented all around you is like treasure hunting—and you never know when you might strike gold.

TREND TIP 3

Don't Forget Psych 101

In some ways, of all the tips you will be given in this book, the most crucial one is to factor in how human behavior can drive trends. You can apply this fundamental insight in many trend-spotting ways. No matter how sensible it may seem to invest in a product or service, ultimately all trends are dependent on human nature—which is not always logical. I am the first to admit it: humans often don't act in their own best interest. How many of us are told by the doctor to watch our cholesterol, but still order the strip steak and chocolate mousse? How many of us are on a budget, but still use our credit cards to buy ourselves that trip to the Bahamas (hard to turn down that bargain airfare, we justify!) or those pricey playoff tickets?

These patterns start young. I recall fellow students struggling to pay off college loans, but still shopping for jewelry and clothes at Tiffany and Saks. They didn't have the money, but they just couldn't resist. As a result, some of us live in debt for much of our lives and spend huge sums servicing that debt. Many of us struggle to tame our spending habits, but we'd rather be in debt and have a good meal, the next big thing in cell phones, a new outfit, or a vacation than put on the brakes.

I am clearly speaking in generalizations. No two individuals are the same. I went to the movies last week—the reviews had all dubbed the film a rollicking comedy—yet I sat through the entire two hours and didn't laugh once. That said, the row of people sitting in front of me could hardly breathe, they were laughing so hard. What tickles other people's funny bones is not the same as what tickles mine. What makes me turn my head is often going to be different from what makes the next guy turn his head.

That said, fortunately for the trend spotter looking to make money, certain universal human behaviors do seem to remain constant over time, and we can turn to them to discover trends. I've made good money from spotting trends I realized were driven by these behaviors.

As I cautioned earlier about applying Six Degrees to trends, understanding human behavior is useful not just in predicting trends, it is also important in realizing that some things will not become trends. Sometimes you spot something that looks like it could turn into a trend, you mull it over logically, and conclude that this is a trend in the making. Yet human behavior should tell you that you probably cannot count on that trend.

Being aware of inherent aspects of human nature that have the power to override factors that might otherwise drive a trend, or to add fuel to a trend's fire, can be a huge help in trend spotting. What are the human behavioral constants that I've observed? Don't worry, I'm not actually going to turn this book into a psychology text. I can sum up the most important ones with the fingers of one hand; and most of them are related to human weaknesses and wish fulfillment.

We All Want to Live Forever

I admit it, I do. Wouldn't it be great to be able to watch your kids grow into sage adults, and your grandkids do the same? Isn't life too precious to let it go? Not wanting to die is one of the deepest, most fundamental of all human impulses. And from the moment that humans learned how to sell things to other humans, people have been capitalizing on this impulse. Whether it was the ancient Chinese selling cinnabar and jade or the ancient Greeks peddling pollywort, there has always been value in a product that proclaims it is the fountain of youth.

As the famous Chinese proverb reads, "An inch of time is an inch of gold, but you can't buy that inch of time with an inch of gold." How true—and yet, generation after generation is willing to try to buy more time. Today more than ever, the life-prolonging industry is booming. Whether it's in the health care sector, with the billions and billions of dollars spent yearly on medications, salves, scans, surgeries; or in the food industry or the fitness field, where money is spent on everything from vitamins to diets to exercise equipment, a great deal of money is being made. A drive to achieve immortality is a particularly potent predictor when coupled with demographic statistics involving the number of aging baby boomers in today's population. Together, you have a real recipe for spotting money-making trends.

At the turn of the twenty-first century, I recognized this trend opportunity. After all, the baby boomers are the largest and most affluent generation in history. And according to social psychologists—not to mention my own, albeit less scientific, observations—they are also highly committed to self-improvement. I knew that around 2010, we'd start having a huge influx of baby boomers retiring. Meanwhile, from my own experiences in aging, I found that things that *used* to be physically easy were suddenly getting harder. Leaning down to pick up my briefcase, I pulled my back. While exercising at the gym, I strained my knee. That sort of thing. Then it hit me—baby boomers would want to feel like they could live forever, but to do that, they would need to remain active as they aged. In order to stay active, they'd be purchasing athletic equipment and gym memberships, and would be needing things like artificial hips and knees.

Playing the Six Degrees game, I thought about how, in addition to wanting to stay in shape, boomers were going to want to stay sexually active. When I heard about Viagra, buying the stock was a no-brainer. It's an unfortunate truth that men lose their sexual potency as they age. And with the growing number of baby boomers getting older, the market for such a drug seemed vast. When the drug was approved by the FDA in less than six months, I knew Pfizer was going to have a field day. It was a solid company with the financial resources to capitalize on a drug of Viagra's caliber, so I invested on the day of approval. Pfizer stock had been climbing pretty steadily for several years previously, but I was confident Viagra was the kind of game changer that would give it a sustained push. The stock nearly doubled within the first year following approval.

In an example of not taking enough account of changing market conditions, what I didn't see coming, but should have, was a similar product put out by Eli Lilly, called Cialis. It pushed its way into the Viagra market and, as it did, I made the mistake of holding onto Pfizer, and watched with dismay as the stock kept dropping, losing half its value in a year. Fortunately it rebounded part of the way, and I took my gain and got out of Pfizer no worse for the wear. This is a sobering reminder that we can never rely on only one key factor for our assessment of a stock's future potential. In this case, the human nature analysis was on target, but competition proved crucial.

Medical products, such as pharmaceuticals or knee replacements (made by companies like Biomet), are only one piece of the immortality trend game. There's also the food we eat, the pills and vitamins we take, the drinks we consume. I could write a whole book about the many types of businesses that will benefit from people's impulse to live forever. For just one of many examples, take a company like Nutraceutical International Corp., which makes, sells, and markets health branded nutritional supplements and other natural products sold through natural food stores. I first identified this as an undervalued small cap stock on my AOL blog in October 2006, when it was trading at $14.

Everywhere I looked I saw signs that the organic health food movement was undergoing a real resurgence in the press and in products offered. Doctors and scientists were publishing articles about the health problems associated with processed foods and pesticide-laden fruits and vegetables, and the news media were covering the story more and more. Not only that, but I personally was wary of the pesticides and additives that go into foods nowadays. I never used to worry, but life and age change us. When possible, I'm buying organic now, and I'm clearly not the only one.

I did my homework and found out that Nutraceutical offered the optimal blend of products for the time, it was one of only two such natural food distributors in the United States, and it was undervalued vis-à-vis its growth potential. The company also had better operating margins than its peers; 15 percent versus less than 12 percent for the competitors. Yet Nutraceutical was trading at a lower and more attractive P/E multiple of 13 while the industry average was a P/E multiple of around 20. At the time of this writing, the stock had jumped from $14 to $17, a gain of more than 20 percent, in just a few months. I think the stock will continue to rise, and I've bought it for the long term.

Fortunately for the many companies and investors out there interested in making money, there are regularly great opportunities for new products and services that try to satisfy our desire to extend life. The reality is, it doesn't matter if the product or service actually prolongs life. It only matters that people *perceive* that it prolongs life. *Pay attention to the headlines* that tell people what will and won't make them live forever—because everyone else is paying attention as well. One day, it's organic food. The next day it's wine and chocolate. The day after, it's jogging. And then it's walking, not jogging.

What will be the "live-longer" headline that grabs people next? It's important to distinguish between flash-in-the-pan fad and a longer trend (as discussed in the next chapter), but whatever the next "live longer" trend may be, I guarantee that people will be willing to spend lots of money on that product. And I equally guarantee that if you remain vigilant to the human drive to live longer, you will be able to make money off many opportunities to come.

We Put Ourselves First

The other day, I was waiting in the long checkout line at the Whole Foods Market near my apartment. It snaked all the way through the salad bar section, doubling back on itself twice. Everyone who approached the line groaned, and as I stood patiently with my basket, I observed no less than seven people try to "slip" their way into the front of the line. It has always been clear to me that people, by nature, are mildly selfish, and this behavior only drove it home further. Ours is an ego-driven culture. We live in a culture where we tend to put ourselves and our families first. Like it or not. Admit to it or not. And even when we put others first, we sneak ourselves into the equation as a close second! Some scientists have even gone so far as to say that selfishness is encoded in our DNA.

Ego is a very strong catalyst for trends. A quick glance at the thriving spa culture or the heavy reliance on personal therapy, and you see how egos play a strong role in driving business and trends. Look at the proliferation of self-published memoirs and people dying to get on reality television shows. Companies know this, and they profit from it. So can you.

Let's look at the automotive industry. Nothing exemplifies the sales power of egos more than cars, to my mind. Most cars work the same, roughly speaking. Most provide roughly equal safety: nowadays, most are equipped with air bags and have strong exterior shells to withstand collisions fairly well. They all get us from point A to point B, and can travel at high speeds when the pedal is pushed to the metal. They are all perfectly comfortable. The other day, I was riding in a friend's lower-end-model Honda Civic, and my seat was more comfortable than the seats in my other friend's luxury-model Jaguar. If all cars nowadays offer the same basic features, why are people willing to spend huge amounts for some cars? Of course, the answer is that many people want to be seen driving the latest in luxury, because it shows they are powerful and wealthy.

For some time, marketers in the automotive field aimed their advertising efforts squarely at the male ego. I noticed they were missing a growing trend. Women, like men, are increasingly ego driven when it comes to their cars—yet they still need to fit the 2.4 kids, the soccer balls, and the groceries. I discovered this myself when, in 1991, I was finishing my MBA at Wharton. I wrote a thesis on what BMW needed to create as its next-generation automobile. I performed market research and correlated the thousands of data points I collected from surveys and focus groups. It became empirically clear that the baby boomers were making good money, and had lots of children to transport. In the end, I recommended to BMW that they build an SUV. Unlike past efforts, they should focus their advertising on the female ego. I explained that the "woman of the family" would be making buying decisions in the future—she'll be providing more and more of the family's money—and she wasn't interested in the latest boring minivan. BMW had the brand potential to be known as much more than a "guy car." They could create a "luxury family vehicle" that crossed the gender divide.

I had a meeting with some executives at the BMW of North America headquarters. They listened to the presentation and laughed at me. In the end, the company lost the opportunity to be one of the first to market with a luxury

SUV, and ultimately the Land Cruiser and Range Rover gained momentum as the popular high-end family vehicles.

Why do we humans have the notion that the more we spend on ourselves, the more we are of worth? Leave the answer to psychologists; all you and I need to know as trend spotters is that this impulse is strong. There's no end to how it manifests itself. Look at the wedding industry. Each year, happy couples celebrate their love in excessive, lavish parties, often breaking the bank in order to make their wedding a worthy display of their love. A recent study found that the average wedding in America costs more than $26,000, and the business is estimated to be a more than $50 billion industry.

And look at the newborn-baby business; we're spending more than $10 billion per year on all those clothes to make our infants and toddlers as cute as possible. Do you think Junior, at three months old, really notices that his booties are made of cashmere? Of course not, but the next-door neighbor might. And the trend spotter who wants to invest in a solid baby company—whether it be organic foods, new toys, clothing products, or baby accessories—might as well. I for one buy only organic food for my baby, and from talking to other mothers, I realize I'm not alone. In fact, it always seems to be sold out at Whole Foods. This is one of the reasons why I think the maker of my baby's food, Hain Celestial Group, the leading natural and organics food maker in the United States, is a winner. And at the time of this writing, I've already made money off the stock.

We Are Vain

The link between ego and vanity is clear. Just as we work hard to maintain a strong sense of self-worth, most of us try to look our best. Never forget, when looking for investment opportunities, that vanity sells products and services. It is the underpinning to nearly all the advertising in the glossy magazines. From blushers to blow-dries, we spend more money than we probably can afford trying to make ourselves look good. Many trends are propelled by this human impulse, and advertisers are more aware of this than anyone else. Look at how fashion magazines draw attention to what celebrities wear, how they style their hair, how they paint their nails. Look at plastic surgery rates rising throughout the country. Look at how much people are willing to pay for a designer T-shirt.

While an intense commitment to looking good was once the strongest preoccupation of women, it has spilled full force into the world of men. The media has seized on this fact, and as it gets played out in the pages of magazines and on TV, more men become conscious of things only women used to care about. I know plenty of businessmen on Wall Street who spend a fortune on manicures, the latest cut of suit, and a fancy haircut. And they would be the first to admit it. After all, they learned to do it in the pages of *GQ*.

Keep in mind that *you'll be able to make money by remembering that emotion is always stronger than reason in driving consumption*. By keeping sight of this basic feature of human nature, you can often understand why some trends take off while others do not. For example, there is a trend today toward natural foods and wholesome products. One might think that this trend would spill into how we look, but it doesn't. The use of beauty and hair products made from chemicals is at an all-time high, not to mention the incidence of plastic surgery. Even the word "plastic" screams of the unnatural. In Hollywood, celebrities who are donating money to environmental causes and going vegan and buying only locally grown, organic foods are also paying a pretty penny to have silicone injected into their lips, for example. Yes, it is hypocritical. But it is happening in droves. And it is not just limited to the stars in Hollywood. A friend of mine recently shared a story of her friend, a woman who is as "crunchy granola" as they come. She eats only organic foods; she lives on a farm with her two children. Everyone in the family is dressed in all-natural fibers. And yet, at age forty, she decided she was sick of the wrinkles appearing on her face, and to everyone's shock, she had a face lift. That vanity could overwhelm the patterns in this woman's life just goes to show how powerful a human impulse it is.

How do we capitalize on the human impulse of vanity? Pay attention to changes in style. Let's take a company like Mentor. This company produces implants for breast augmentation. Anybody who stood in line in a grocery store anytime in the early twenty-first century would be hard pressed not to notice that every magazine in the rack featured smiling women with large, perfect breasts. Gone were the images from the '90s of wafer-thin Kate Moss types.

Breasts were back in style. Now imagine you went home, as I did one day, and looked into solidly run companies that make breast implants. You would have found Mentor. This company, whose annual report cover boasted, "because bigger is better," made the next-generation breast implant and didn't carry the baggage of the once-popular silicone, which is alleged to have health risks. If in 2003 you had invested, say, $1,000 in the stock when it was trading at $20, you'd now have nearly $2,000 at the time of writing this book. Its stock price has nearly doubled in four years.

Vanity is tied in many ways to the next basic truth to keep in mind. We believe that if we spend on our appearance, we will be happy. And the search for happiness is, after all, the root of most of our impulses.

We Seek the Promise of Happiness

We all want to be happy. Over time, the forces at work in our culture have turned us into avid consumers of products and services we believe will make us happier. We spend money lavishly to be happy—or more correctly, on the *promise* of being happy. Advertisers are smart about suggesting that a product or service holds the promise of making us happy. Don't ever forget the lengths that people will go to, and the money they will spend, to find happiness. Will it be found in a religion? In improving their appearance? In owning more things? In buying something luxurious? In buying something that promises them love?

We all know that, too often, people attribute happiness, or the lack of it, to their appearance. They convince themselves that if only they could lose ten pounds, they would be happy. If only their nose weren't so big, they'd be happy. If only they didn't have love handles or saddlebags, their lives would be perfect.

But it doesn't end there. It isn't just with our physical appearance that we try to buy happiness; it's also about the goods we buy. Take accessories. We all love the feeling of luxury, and we like it even more when it's affordable. We think that the purchase of luxury will bring us happiness. Companies like Coach and Estee Lauder have made millions from this innate desire for beauty and luxury. Of course, in making use of this insight, you have to know which brands have strong companies behind them. For example, at the time of writing this book, Coach has been rising steadily for nearly five years, while Estee Lauder has been up and down quite a bit in the same time period, and its earnings have been declining.

One reason for the difference is that there are many more cosmetics makers than there are luxury leather producers, so Coach is able to dominate in a way Estee Lauder isn't. (Though Estee Lauder has done much better of late, with brands like Aveda and Bobbi Brown that are seen as much more hip.) Before rushing out to buy the stock of your favorite accessory, make sure you do your research and get a sense of the company's earnings and historical stock prices which reflect the company's ability to benefit from market conditions.

Sometimes it's not the product itself, but the experience of consuming and the promise of happiness offered that drives us. Several years ago, I went through a personal rough patch and was feeling blue. While waiting in line at the deli, my eye caught the scratch-to-win lottery tickets. I never play the lottery, but now, the promise offered by winning big was exactly the kind of pick-me-up I needed. My buying scratch tickets that day was a textbook example of why casinos and lotteries are so popular. I was buying some *hope*. Despite all evidence pointing to the very low likelihood of *making* money, and the very high likelihood of *losing* money, people love the rush they get from the promise of gambling. Tied to this is the human impulse to compete and win. For this reason, casinos are perennial winners and traditionally make good long-term investments. Take Harrah's Entertainment, a chain of casinos and hotels, for example. Now up in the $80 range, this stock shows no signs of slowing. Sure, there are dips, but in general, the allure of buying happiness and the human drive to win, coupled with a solid business, is a recipe for success.

Another example of buying into the promise of happiness is the cruise line industry. Royal Caribbean Cruise Line is a strong company that has benefited from its promise of a stress-free, luxurious vacation. But be careful with investing in cruise lines and other *cyclical stocks*—stocks that are tied closely to up and down cycles in the economy. When people aren't feeling flush, they tend to cut expenses like cruises from their budgets before they cut things like groceries and gambling. You should buy these stocks when the economy is bad and the stocks are down, then wait for the economy to turn around again, when they will pretty reliably rise in price once more. Similarly, you need to make sure to sell them when the economy is good; you won't want to, because they'll be reporting strong revenues, but it's better to get out a bit early on cyclical stocks and take your gain, rather than waiting too long and getting nothing.

We All Want to Belong

We are lemmings. Trends wouldn't exist at all were it not for this basic human impulse. Most of us try our hardest not to stand out, yet paradoxically, at the same time, we want to have something better than everyone else has. Americans have taken "keeping up with the Joneses" to a whole new level ever since the boom of the 1980s. It's why we drive more and more BMWs and Mercedes, and it's why our houses keep getting bigger and bigger. It's all about being part of the crowd—part of the elite crowd, that is.

Don't confuse this tendency with the pure desire for luxury; the need to belong is more about the desire to be *seen* having luxury items than the desire to *have* luxury items. Tiffany is a company that has marketed brilliantly to capitalize on this desire. What could be more recognizable than Tiffany blue? When you give someone a gift in one of those boxes, they know immediately that you've gone all out. If you're walking down the street carrying one of those shopping bags, people will notice you from a block away. Or consider Louis Vuitton, especially in comparison to Coach. You buy a Coach bag because you want the sumptuous leather and some up-market appeal. You buy a Louis Vuitton bag because you want nice leather, but even more because that elegant "LV" pattern is going to draw jealous stares from other women.

We will pay a premium for products and services that are marks of membership in an elite tribe. As a result, these luxury manufacturers can command top dollar and, often, they have high profit margins that help drive their businesses and make them good stocks to own.

We Crave a Moral Center

Morals sell. While we are always out for ourselves, we all need to feel we have a moral compass; it's human nature, and it helps us sleep at night. Morals are also big business. From religion to self-help books to twelve-step programs to charities, people pour their money into causes that they feel make them better people. A great example of how this impulse plays out in trends is the post-9/11 movement toward what is termed "conscience commerce." Basically, conscience commerce is a term to describe businesses that help a charity or cause, usually by donating a portion of proceeds from product sales to the cause. Conscience-commerce companies benefit from several of the human desires highlighted in this chapter. While people like to put themselves first, and they want to buy things to try to achieve happiness, they also want to feel good about themselves and they don't want to think they are self-centered.

Many businesspeople today are taking another look at their lives and deciding to pursue a calling that would make money *and* give back to the community. For example, many entrepreneurs set up sports leagues where the participants pay an entrance fee that goes to a charity.

Investing with an eye to this morals trend is tricky, though. Many of these companies are too small or too new to be publicly traded, so there aren't many in which one can invest. Also, few of the publicly traded companies engaged in morals-based marketing have charitable or altruistic efforts as their main focus. More and more, though, companies are emphasizing sustainable growth, or have "green" business practices, or make substantial donations to good causes. It can take a bit of research to figure out how to invest in a conscious-commerce way, but there are plenty of mutual funds that do this, engaging in what is known as "socially responsible investing." These funds save you time by doing the company-by-company research you'd have to do to figure out which companies reflect your values.

You can invest in funds, for example, that avoid corporations with poor environmental records. These funds are easy to find on the internet—just search for "socially responsible investing." You can research them and figure out which are the highest performing and appeal most to your values. There are some expenses involved, of course, like with every other mutual fund, but you can view that as a donation of sorts (though don't try claiming a tax deduction for it!).

Many who want to invest in socially responsible ways are also drawn to religious-based funds. There's no doubt that religion remains an important, if not central, part of the vast majority of Americans' lives. As with socially responsible investing, it is difficult to find companies with religion as their primary goal, but there are, say, Catholic funds like the Ave Maria Mutual Funds and the Aquinas Funds at Luther King Capital Management, which aim to promote Catholic family values at the same time that they strive to provide solid returns to their investors.

As I mentioned, at this point there aren't a lot of stocks that capitalize purely on the desire for us to do and be good (there are no publicly traded churches!). But this is nevertheless a basic human behavioral trend for us to watch for. As companies begin to strive as hard to be moral as they do to make profits, you may be able to make money in a righteous way.

Always keep these simple Psych 101 tips in mind when evaluating trends. They will help you to anticipate better which nascent trends will take off and which might fizzle. As mentioned earlier, you might expect that news reports about potential dangers of silicone would severely hurt makers of breast implants. And yet, humans are vain creatures, and the demand has remained steady, so implant maker Mentor continues to thrive.

Tips aside, I think a truly powerful—and easy—rule of thumb is to look at yourself honestly and consider how *you* react to things. Your behavior is likely not much different from that of the guy next door or the woman twenty states over. What do you want? What would you do and how would you act when confronted with an idea, product, or service? Oftentimes, your answer will be right on the money, as long as you're really telling yourself the truth.

TREND TIP 4

Learn When a Spade Is a Spade

When the Obvious Trend Is Still Worth Riding, and When It Is Just a Fad

We're all familiar with the "looks too good to be true" phenomenon—and most of us are wary enough not to get burned by it. The *No Money Down* mortgage! The *You Have Won a Free Trip to the Bahamas!* postcard. Clearly, there is a catch, right? We read the fine print, and more times than not, we find we're correct. Maybe the hitch is that there is an absurd interest rate on the mortgage, or the

Bahamas trip is free—once you've put yourself on a mailing list and then been chosen from millions out of a huge hat. No question, there is a good reason to be suspicious of things that *must* have a catch.

It's not any different in investing. Hype over a stock gets built up, and the careful investor questions if something *that obvious* could possibly be a good value. When the tech craze was in full force, people were singing the praises of companies like theglobe.com, an online community, or Flooz.com, which proposed an entire new, internet-only currency. If I had been a lemming and followed the herd without doing my homework, I might have jumped in and bought shares of theglobe.com after its extraordinary IPO, which opened at $9 and was over $63 on its first day of trading. It never went much higher, and in less than three years the stock was worth 14 cents. If I'd invested after that stellar first day, I would have lost quite a bit of money. Of course, I never would have had a chance to invest in Flooz, as it went belly-up before making it to an IPO. I still find myself chuckling over some of the crazy ideas from the late 1990s dot-com craze.

Or, back in early 2000, everyone was eating Krispy Kreme doughnuts and the stock was at $50. It seemed like Krispy Kreme was some big secret, and if you were in on it, that made you hip and cool. But what was the real trend here? This was a faddish brand, more than anything (coupled with a good excuse to eat a doughnut and feel hip!). Then Krispy Kreme became overexposed, sold in grocery stores and, even worse, at the highway convenience stores.

Quickly the brand lost its luster, the sense that these were special food items, rare and cool as albino elephants. At the same time, the Atkins diet (another fad, as most diets are) said no to carbs, and within eighteen months Krispy Kreme had dropped to $10.

Hype can be infectious. Once you get the bug, it can cloud your judgment. But sometimes a spade *is* indeed a spade. In the world of trends, we like to think that the first person to identify the trend is the real winner. But I've found, more times than not, that when a trend is lasting and strong, getting in on the game a bit later isn't going to hurt you. Yes, the payout might be greater for the first spotter of a trend, but *a trend rider who rides the wave a bit later can still make out just fine*. If you had bought Google.com during its IPO in August 2004 at $85, you would have done better than had you invested in the company four months later, at $180. But two years later, with Google's stock soaring at $468, you would have been a winner either way. Bottom line: just because others are already talking about a stock, don't assume that it isn't a good investment anymore.

I like to say that *if there is a sound explanation for the excitement, don't shy away from the investment*. Once again, using Google as an example, everyone was buzzing about Google when it was about to go public in 2004. It offered a service that couldn't be beaten. How many people did you know who used Google as their home page? It was the great "discovery" that had already been discovered, and everyone wanted to turn their friends, family, and coworkers on to it. This clearly wasn't a product that would disappear—and it was growing and getting more sophisticated by the day.

But it also clearly was already known by everyone and their mother, and people worried that it was another example of 1990s tech hype. Many people I know hesitated to invest in the IPO for that reason. They ignored what they saw with their own eyes and heard with their own ears—the obvious fact that Google was providing a superior service. To wit, this company was clearly flexible, adaptable, and eminently creative, but many investors feared another burst bubble, and as a result they didn't jump on the IPO. If they had bought 10 shares then, for $850, as of early 2007 their investment would be worth more than $4,500.

As always, it's important to do your research when a company seems hyped, discovered, and obvious, to make sure there is evidence of a solid trend wave to ride. But acting on *valid* hype is a sound trends strategy. These trends won't generally yield blockbuster results unless you're in on them early enough, or unless you play the Six Degrees game and jump on a tangentially related trend. But they will yield results all the same.

When investing in companies getting lots of hype, a key assessment you must make is to evaluate whether the buzz indicates a fad or a longer-term trend. If I had a dime for every fad that I've observed build to a frenzied crescendo, only to fizzle out within months, I'd be rich just from that. Look at kids' products, for instance. Gummy bracelets were a fad in the '80s, Pokemon in the '90s. And a fad today, at the time of writing this book, is Bratz dolls. How do you tell the difference? This is tricky, but I can offer some good rules of thumb. One indicator is that fads often involve promises that are too good to be true, or some extreme change in taste or behavior. Trends, by contrast, tend to be related to more plausible fundamental changes in the way we or companies operate. Trends therefore tend to spread out into a broader range of products and services. For example, the organic trend has been powerful enough to cause biotech companies like Monsanto to change their marketing, and it's spawned an increasing array of foods and stores that cater specifically to this demand. Both the Atkins diet and organics were premised on helping us live better, but one had staying power while the other was unrealistic for us to stick to over time. In assessing a potential trend, focus on determining if it's likely to stick in our culture for a long or a short time. If you think it's likely to be popular for only a short time, it's probably a fad. A diet, a fashion, a way of thinking that isn't grounded in anything meaningful, lasting, or sustainable—these are usually indicators of fads. I mean, how many of us really believed we could live the rest of our lives without eating pasta and bread on a regular basis?

Another good rule of thumb is the pervasiveness of an apparent trend. If the buzz about it is out of New York or Los Angeles, but no one in the Midwest has even heard about it, it may be too early in the trend for most investors or possibly just a flash in the pan. Lasting trends are widespread. Before Google's IPO, it wasn't just techies in Silicon

Valley using the search engine for their web queries; there were plenty of people using it in Nebraska as well.

What if, in doing your research, you determine that the buzz is misguided? In other words, if you identify that the hype is over a company or a trend that simply doesn't have lasting power? There may still be good money to be made by investing in that trend. Both fads and trends can be exploited to make a profit—you just need to be careful about evaluating and closely monitoring which you're dealing with. The long-term trend you ride for the long haul, the fad you get in and out of quickly. During the Atkins craze, short-term investments in meat suppliers, for example, probably wouldn't have been a terrible idea, provided the companies had solid fundamentals.

Investing in a fad is a riskier investment that takes that much more careful monitoring, because it involves your buying and holding a stock for the very short term, and jumping off before others figure out that the trend or company is overhyped. *If you're going to invest in fads, make sure you are watching the clock—and get out in time in order to make, not lose, money.*

While I've personally found that this strategy can yield consistent and sizable returns, you need the stomach for this type of riskier, short-term investment. This type of investing also carries the risk of the short-term capital gains tax hit I discussed earlier. Therefore I don't recommend this type of in-and-out investment for everyone. It's crucial to know your time horizon. Are you willing and able to put this money at risk with the big-wave surfers? If not, then it's perfectly okay to avoid those waves altogether and just wait watchfully for the plenty of other decent-size waves to come along.

So as I stressed before, the safer strategy is to identify which buzz is directed at *lasting trends*, rather than at flashes in the pan. Take the environment and the growing recognition that our country has to develop meaningful energy alternatives in order to stave off global warming and wean ourselves off dependency on foreign oil from unsavory regimes. No question, this concern is being hyped to the hilt at the time of my writing this book. But take a closer look: It's eminently clear that this is not just a fad. The environment is going downhill fast, and in order to try to save it, people are going to have to start to adopt new technologies and new personal practices. Even though this is obvious to many people already, putting money in shares of solid companies that are also stewards of the environment is still a good bet. Even better is putting money in solid companies with new environmental ideas or technology that might help save us all.

Back in late 2002, a friend from California was telling me about the water issues out there. I'd seen *Chinatown* and knew the "water wars" went way back to the beginning of the twentieth century, but I never thought about water issues as a potential investment until my friend told me how tight the supplies were, and described the political and economic battles being waged between the various interest groups—farmers, cities, golf courses, you name it—claiming their share of this valuable commodity. I poked around and found a company called Tetra Tech that does consulting and engineering work in water resource management. This seemed a company that was doing the right thing environmentally, and was dealing with a resource with a great deal of financial significance. So I bought the stock at about $7 and cheered as it soared to $25 in little more than a year. Since then it's been up and down, but at $22 my investment has still more than tripled in value. I continue to hold it because I believe this company is doing the right thing, and that its services will only grow more important as water resources diminish and as our nation becomes increasingly attuned to environmental issues.

You can't have a conversation about buzz, fads, and lasting trends without hitting on the issue of technology and gadgets. We all know how technology comes and goes. Cassette tapes disappeared when CDs came around; now Tower Records is shuttering its stores because of competition from online music sales. It's always a risky endeavor to invest in technology, but sometimes you know when a product is truly revolutionary.

Take the BlackBerry (made by Research In Motion). I was intrigued by the device when it first came out in the late 1990s. Of course I had one, like everyone else in finance. But I didn't buy the stock then, as I wasn't sure how far the reach would go without phone service as a feature. When the company integrated a phone into their email system, and every single banker I knew was talking about it, I knew the BlackBerry had something with truly mass appeal. It had already been discovered and hyped, but now I knew it was going to be around for a long time. I bought this stock in early 2003, when it was in the low teens. I knew there would be competition, and even figured it would come from Palm, but the basic appeal of the BlackBerry versus the Palm was undeniable. Since then the Research In Motion stock has climbed above $215, and the biggest question is when to sell. (At the time of writing this, Apple had just begun selling the iPhone. Will this be the threat that will finally knock BlackBerry off its throne? I'll be keeping a close eye on it.)

While the BlackBerry was a perfect example of a tech spade that is a spade—an obvious lasting trend—the Segway is an example of a hyped, short-lived tech fad. Before it was finally unveiled in 2001, the hype was at an all-time high. It was obvious that no one would "discover" this company; you couldn't turn on the radio or open a newspaper without hearing about it. This was a mysterious new invention that was said would revolutionize not only the way humans traveled, but the way cities would be designed in the future. And who knows, perhaps the makers of the world's first self-balancing personal transportation device will end up proving they were right, but in the near future, the technology simply isn't practical to succeed in a big way. You can't use the devices on the crowded sidewalks of New York City, for instance, a place where they were expected to sell strongly. As fun as they might be to drive, there is no way to use them for long distances, or in the rain, or safely on the roads. This meant the suburbs and countryside were out, too. In short, it wasn't a practical enough concept to last. So as quickly as the buzz had built up, it died. This spade was *not* a spade, it would seem.

The Obvious Factor Meets the Obsolete Factor

I travel a lot for business. Ten years ago, when I needed to take a trip, I'd call up my local travel agent and have her arrange my flight and hotel plans. As of last year, I've stopped communicating with her. Don't get me wrong: she is a wonderful and helpful woman. But after Expedia.com started their service under Microsoft's aegis in 1996, I found that I was using the site more and more. Not only were their prices much better, they also allowed me to take my schedule into my own hands. While I didn't have any money invested in my travel agent (except for all the money I threw into her business for my traveling), had her company been public and I owned shares, I'd be sure to have sold them the day I discovered online booking.

If a service or product *seems* outmoded, it probably *is* outmoded. Again, sometimes a spade *is* a spade! For every trend moving forward, there is a trend that is sputtering out. You may have ditched your clunky CD burner, for instance—your new computer has a built-in burner, and it's much easier to download music online anyway. Dump stock in companies that are not keeping up with technology. They will eventually be swept out to sea on the receding tide, and you don't want your money swept with them.

A perfect example of this is Eastman Kodak. In 1998 they were flying high, perhaps the premier camera company of their time, with a stock price over $80. Founded in 1881, Kodak built a name for itself as a solid company with a quality product. I owned Kodak cameras my whole life, and I always used their services to develop my film. But by 1999, with the introduction of the Nikon D1, times were about to change in a big way for the rest of the world: the proliferation of the digital camera was upon us. Even though the first mass-market digital cameras were expensive, I found myself with one anyway: friends had them, and when I borrowed their cameras, I saw that these were the real deal. They were a cinch to use, they took great photos, and you didn't need to pay to develop the film. What's more, you didn't need to worry about wasting film. I remember the first time using a digital camera at a wedding, I took something like 275 photographs of the bride! I never would have done this with traditional 35-millimeter film. It simply would have cost too much to develop.

It was obvious to me that in time, the whole world would be going digital. If only it had been as obvious to Kodak. They'd been early to the game of digital photography, but had never pursued it as a primary focus. For whatever reason, they stuck to the traditional model of photography, relying on their bread and butter, the film and film development business, to carry them forward. This was a tide that was going out, out, out.

By 2003, Kodak shares were down around $20. This was 25 percent off their price of just a few years earlier.

Sadly, in 2004, they were forced to lay off about 12,000 to 15,000 people. A cost-savings effort caused their stock to regain some ground, getting up to $35 by the end of the year, before the price dropped once again into the $20s in early 2005. Thankfully I had dumped the stock at around $60 back in 2000, when I first bought a digital camera. I may have been a bit late to drop it—more sharp-eyed technology aficionados might have known to get out of Kodak in 1998 or 1999—but I cut loose as soon as it became obvious that Kodak was missing out on the action.

Even if you're a little late to notice the obvious, you can still make money (or cut a loss), as long as you act on your observations and convictions. Many other investors won't be quite as savvy, and will ride a company like Kodak to the bottom, especially because of its well-known name. Again, this is another example of being vigilant about watching for change and not falling in love with any stock you own.

No Man Is an Island

While it is important to be aware of the obvious things that other people are excited about, in the world of riding trends it's equally important to be attuned to your own obvious preferences. Simply put, unless you have truly offbeat taste, the things you love may well become trends, if they aren't already. I can't stress this point enough. Many of the long-term, solid trends I've identified in the past, and ridden to great financial success, are products or services that I found myself relying on.

In the late 1990s, for example, I found myself obsessed with coffee. I'd always been a coffee drinker, but I took a trip to Italy and, more than ever before, really enjoyed espresso, lattes, macchiatos, and other coffee drinks I could find only after meals at Italian restaurants or at specialty coffee houses in Greenwich Village. And the appeal was as much about the atmosphere surrounding the drink as it was the drink itself. Then I heard about a company called Starbucks, which was taking coffee culture from Seattle and turning it into an everyday pleasure. Knowing how much I enjoyed these coffees, I invested in Starbucks in 1998, when it was still below $10. I knew it was a business that made many of its sales in increments of $2 or $3 (or less), and it wasn't yet clear that the rest of America would take to coffee in the same way. But it was as plain as day to me! As you can imagine, I have made a very substantial profit in the company.

A friend of mine loves to brag about having been into Skype before anyone else she knows. When her new boyfriend moved to London, she discovered love wasn't cheap. Her long-distance bills were so high that she realized she could have bought two round-trip tickets a month for the amount she was spending to talk to him on the phone. Then a blogger she read turned her on to Skype, which you may now know all about: a service easily downloaded onto your computer, for free, that allows you to talk over the internet using a headset. Quickly, she found that she was rarely using her traditional phone. Skype service was just as clear as, if not better than, her normal phone, and it was not just cheap, it was often free! So she canceled her traditional long-distance service from Verizon. What was more, she told her parents about the service, along with friends, and they were converts as well.

Unfortunately, my friend was never able to invest in Skype, though she probably would have made a fortune if she had. As the rumors grew during 2005 about a possible Skype IPO, eBay swept in and bought the young company for $2.6 billion. My friend certainly got some satisfaction at having her instincts proven right, but she didn't actually get to act on them.

Simply put, invest in things that have become trends in your own life. If you love a product or service and find yourself using it and depending on it, chances are that other people likely feel the same way—and the company responsible for the product or service is poised to do well.

As with everything, the converse plays into investment strategy as well. If you think a product or service is ridiculous or falling out of fashion, listen to yourself: it likely won't become a trend, or will trend downward.

The key point to Trend Tip 4 is to anticipate the staying power of a trend or the fad, the length of time you think the product, service, or general idea will be "hot" (or not), and invest accordingly. And as always, do your research. A company must first and foremost be solid before you put a penny toward it.

TREND TIP 5

Be a News Junkie

Trends Are Reported, Broadcast, and Beamed from Everywhere

In order to pick up on trends early, and to get early word of when trends are peaking, you need to be an avid follower of the news: *The New York Times*, CNN, the BBC, *The Economist*, *Time* magazine, and so on. I subscribe to a wealth of publications. I know what you're thinking: there isn't time in the day to digest all this information. The good news is that you don't have to: by glancing at the headlines (most of them you can get for free online), you are able to gain a general sense of where things are trending. The purpose is not necessarily to listen to the advice or analysis of the pundits, but to know which common themes these headlines tend to discuss. You'll be surprised at what you can learn and how far ahead of the curve you can get.

The news clues you into issues and events not just in politics, but also in business, public perception, and innovation, which both reflect and drive trends. That is, the news tells you what's happening, but it also shapes public perception and therefore also helps to shape what *will* happen. Big and small—from world conflicts, to treaties and trade agreements, to tiny special-interest pieces—you can pick up ideas about trends that might be either building or starting to fall off, as well as learning new insights about current trends.

Take, for instance, parents' concern over internet safety and their children. Over the past several years, I have been noticing articles about how worried parents are about the adult content their children are exposed to on the internet. They are especially nervous that predators might find their children through the web. Then in 2006 the scandal revolving around Congressman Mark Foley sending sexually explicit internet instant messages to congressional pages broke. What made this story stand out more than other stories about internet predators was that he was a respected politician, one who had even spoken out about the dangers of child predators. The revelation sent already concerned parents over the edge. If you couldn't trust this public official, who *could* you trust?

I noticed that a concurrent article in *The Wall Street Journal* discussed how the Foley scandal led to a surge in demand for privacy-software programs. While most of these were sold by well-established companies, and they were not offering new programs (parental monitoring software has been around for years), the Foley scandal showed how one incident can kick a trend into high gear. The article gave a list of companies that were innovators in safety software and internet blocks that helped safeguard children from certain kinds of content.

When I come across lists of companies like this, as I mentioned earlier I keep notes on my BlackBerry. For those companies that are already public, I'll do my research and consider investing. In the case of the *WSJ* article about internet software, some of the companies were not yet public, and I flagged them as ones to research and keep an eye on.

Flagging nonpublic companies brings me to a point I've mentioned before but that's worth emphasizing: *Sometimes the best opportunities in trend watching are found in start-up companies that are clearly onto a trend.* Make a note of them. Throw them into a file, and keep an eye on them over time. Usually, if I've identified the company as strong and innovative, and it seems to be heading down the right path—riding a nascent trend—more times than not, it will eventually go public. When they make their initial IPO, you can snap up shares that may end up paying off in a big way in the long run. I keep a huge folder of companies that I've flagged as promising but are not yet public. Some of the best bargains I have found were first acquired at the IPO of a promising start-up.

Now, it's worth mentioning here that IPO stocks are not easy to get your hands on, as the shares are offered first to large institutions. And more important, IPOs often embody hype, because the company at that point has hired investment banks and PR firms to pump its story (since by law, the company itself is not allowed to do so). IPOs are big waves that should be surfed only by investors who can stomach the big-wave risks associated with them. It's important to remember to be smart about the money you're investing, and it's okay not to invest where and when everyone else is investing. As I've said before, you can make enough money getting in on an IPO a bit later. Having said that, IPO waves can be big, and the payoff can sure be big, too.

One of my most successful IPO purchases was eBay, which I bought when it went public back in 1998. It's hard to remember now, but that IPO was far from a sure thing. There were concerns about the quality of eBay's service, and the IPO market at the time was unstable. A number of analysts went on record with their doubts about how the stock would fare. But I'd been following the company since I first started using the site in the mid-1990s after I read about it in the news, and I was convinced eBay was revolutionary and was brilliantly exploiting the inefficiencies of the market for used goods. I've bought so many things through eBay I can't even remember what my first purchase was. Knowing how unique this company was, how fast it was growing, and how solid the company was financially (backed by premier venture capitalists), I went in at the IPO, buying $20,000 of shares at $16—still a real gamble, despite all my homework. I should have sold when it hit $60 back in early 2005, but I held on a bit too long. I still made a killing, though, selling in early 2006 at $40 a share. This netted me $30,000—and the supreme satisfaction of having been in from the beginning.

I always have my eyes peeled, and I read the business dailies like a hawk. I don't necessarily take the information about specific companies and run out to buy them. I try to step back and see the forest instead of the trees, and to figure out how the smaller bits of information might add up to a larger trend. For example, when I noticed articles about how online retailing was really taking off in 2001 and 2002, I could have bought shares in companies like Amazon. If I had, I would have ended up doing quite well, but at the time I was worried about their profitability. Within those articles about how well the retailers were doing, though, reporters also explained that companies like UPS and, especially, FedEx were having to adjust to a huge growth in demand, because so many purchases were being shipped instead of taken home from a retail store. As I mentioned in the previous chapter about hype versus lasting trends, a good trend indicator is when the phenomenon has enough reach and staying power that it causes change even in other industries.

So after seeing several articles about the impact of online retailing on shipping companies, I began thinking about investing in FedEx, which seemed to be the shipper of choice for many of the online retailers. (It didn't hurt, either, that the growth of business in emerging markets would require an increase in corporate demand for international shipping.) As the holiday season drew near in 2002, I saw more articles about the annual nightmare of retail stores packed with eager holiday shoppers; these articles anticipated a significant jump in online sales to shoppers who wanted to avoid the crowds, and I knew the time had come. I bought shares of FedEx in September at $50 a share and sat back and watched as the stock price started growing. I'd missed the bottom by a few dollars, but I didn't care; the company jumped during the fall, no doubt due to holiday demand; then it dropped back in January. I didn't panic, however, as I was thinking to the future and knew from these articles that demand was only going to grow for the foreseeable future. Five years later, the stock was near $120. I'm holding it for a while longer, until I start seeing news about internet sales leveling off.

In scouring the news, I focus on a set of key types of stories and features: political stories, the advertising spaces, the weather page, and of course, most obviously, the business section.

It's All Politics

New policies taking effect, both here and abroad, can have a huge impact on how companies and the public behave and think. From company regulations to trade pacts, the political news is a goldmine for spotting nascent trends. In April 2006, for example, I was writing a story on green investing in recognition of Earth Week. I discovered that the Environmental Protection Agency (EPA) had recently enforced some fairly stringent laws regarding air pollution. In researching the legislation, I realized that any company that assisted other companies in reducing nitrous oxide and sulfur dioxide emissions would greatly benefit from these new regulations. I investigated further and came across Fuel Tech, a company that offered ways of increasing combustion without increasing emissions. At the time the stock was selling around $15, and in less than a year it had nearly doubled, to above $29. At that point, I could have taken my 100 percent profit and run, but this investment is a long-term keeper for me. I expect that environmental regulations will be getting more and more stringent as time goes on, and with tighter pollution controls, coupled with a highly effective product, I'm confident that Fuel Tech will become a better and better investment.

Another business sector in which regulations can have dramatic effects is pharmaceuticals. The Food and Drug Administration (FDA) may be the government agency that wields the greatest impact on the fortunes of major American companies. When the FDA approves a drug for use, the company making that drug often stands to make a fortune. Of course, there are thousands and thousands of seemingly promising drugs in the research and development pipelines, and not all these drugs will become big hits. In addition, patents eventually expire, and there's an increasing threat from generic-drug makers that has made the pharmaceutical business much less reliable in recent years.

Investing in companies in these patent-reliant and regulated businesses requires vigilance and homework to make sure you're aware of exactly when those patents expire and how many generic-drug companies are poised to jump on that drug.

So you can't just throw your money into any company that has a drug about to be approved. But if you do the research and pay attention to what's getting approved, you can make quite a bit of money by following what the FDA does—or is reportedly about to do.

For example, back in February 2002, I saw a CNN segment with Paula Zahn talking to a plastic surgeon about the impending approval of an anti-wrinkling drug. I knew many women who were starting to worry about their aging skin and spend tons of money on anti-wrinkle creams, but didn't want to go under the knife. As I listened, I knew this product was going to be huge. You've probably guessed by now that the product the surgeon was discussing was Botox. Sure, it had a rather off-putting name—anything with "tox," which is short for "toxin"—and there was something a little scary about putting poison into your skin to ease wrinkling. But it was going to be relatively inexpensive, and minimally invasive, and I was confident that the powerful pull of vanity and the desire for eternal youth would make Botox popular. To me, this was going to be something that wasn't just for Hollywood celebs; it would probably start there, but like so many things it would trickle down. I knew it would be a popular choice early on, for example, with country club women from Greenwich to Houston to Orange County, and I expected interest would continue spreading from there.

So I took a look at Allergan, the company that makes Botox. FDA approval was estimated sometime during that spring of 2002, but I didn't just run out and buy Allergan. The company was trading in the high $30s, and I didn't want to invest at such a seemingly lofty level. So I decided to grab it if the stock dropped below $30. This finally happened about a week before the FDA approval came through. I bought Allergan in the high $20s, thinking I'd surely made my purchase at the bottom.

But Botox didn't gain immediate popularity—I think because there were too many initial concerns about whether people would really want to inject it into their foreheads—and the stock fell to $50. I kicked myself for having bought when I did—but I held on to the shares. In the end, my judgment was correct. Botox did become incredibly popular with a large number of Americans. By 2004, Allergan's stock was near $80; it reached $100 in late 2005, and rose to $120 in early 2007. The biggest question now is whether to sell. My sense is that Botox may not have a great deal more room for growth, and I may indeed get out before the stock evens out or drops. I'll be vigilantly looking for signs of increased competition from other credible providers and slowing growth rates or declining profit margins for Allergan.

As we saw earlier, regulatory bodies like the FDA can

have profound positive effects on the pharmaceutical industry by approving drugs; the converse is also true, of course, and when the FDA kills a drug it can damage, or even kill, a pharmaceutical company. And it's not just the FDA. In the 2004 election, there was much discussion of generic drugs; many citizen groups were pushing for laws that would expand Americans' access to generic drugs from Canada. The drug industry pushed back, of course, knowing that these laws would be disastrous for their revenues. If such a law is ever passed, I'd be very careful about investing in pharmaceuticals until the companies figure out how to deal with the new playing field.

In addition to medicine and the environment, another highly regulated area is the media. The government often makes decisions to prevent or allow mergers, for example, and these decisions often have a huge impact on the shares of media companies. When Congress passed the Telecommunications Act of 1996, which allowed for the multiple ownership of media companies within single markets, this paved the way for an unprecedented roll-up and consolidation of radio ownership. That law changed the face of radio.

I cashed in on the acquisitions that were about to occur by buying into a small and newly formed company called SFX. Entrepreneur Robert F.X. Sillerman created SFX as a vehicle to exploit the changes that the 1996 telecommunications law would bring to radio. SFX purchased 67 radio stations in 1996 alone. Ultimately, SFX was bought by Capstar, and eventually Capstar was bought by Chancellor, which was acquired by Clear Channel, and, as part of the closing deal, I received publicly traded shares in an entity called "SFX Entertainment." My original investment grew tenfold in three years.

I also bought Sirius satellite radio back in 2006, when it was trading at $3, because I read news reports of Mel Karmazin (CEO of Sirius) buying tons of stock and figured he was on to something. I did some more thinking and realized that, in the deregulatory climate of George W. Bush's FCC, Sirius and its archrival XM Radio would eventually discover there wasn't enough room for both of them and would merge to create one powerhouse satellite radio company, combining subscriber bases and cutting costs through economies of scale. Sure enough, in early 2007 the two companies proposed a merger.

Government regulation can often be an investor's friend, so stay tuned to the news coming from the Hill. But with the good comes the bad. Some political actions adversely affect finances, and you need to be wary of these, too. For example, while I am absolutely certain that biofuels and other forms of alternative energy are trends that will only grow for the rest of this century, it's very difficult to know which types of energy and which technologies will be the real winners. The answer will be determined in part by technology, of course. If a solar company can ever make a panel that is small and inexpensive and generates huge amounts of electricity—the big stumbling blocks to solar panels taking off—then the sky will be the limit.

Much of the Green Revolution, and which technologies

will take off, will depend on regulation. Take ethanol, for example. As discussed earlier, concerns about global warming reached a tipping point in 2006, and corn prices shot up as everyone looked to corn ethanol as the new panacea. There's a lot to be said for corn ethanol, but in Brazil they've been making ethanol from sugarcane since the oil crisis of the 1970s. Sugarcane is a cheaper and more efficient way of generating energy than corn, and would almost certainly be more popular here if not for the tariffs that raise the price of Brazilian sugarcane in America. These tariffs, along with other subsidies, help protect the American corn industry, and if the U.S. government ever lifted them, you might see a serious drop in the value of corn and of companies like Archer Daniels Midland. When investing in businesses subject to regulation, you must be on high alert about the ways fortunes may be affected and be a junkie about the news surrounding that regulation.

As with everything, *investor perception is key. Whether or not a bill is passed in Congress can be less important than whether or not investors* believe *a bill is going to be passed.* For instance, as I write, there are jitters on Wall Street that the Democrats, who have regained control of the House and Senate, are going to enact reforms in the prescription benefits of Medicare. Investors are particularly concerned that the Dems are going to alter the law in order to allow the government to negotiate drug prices for Medicare patients, meaning, of course, lower revenue for drug companies. Just the possibility that this might happen sent shares of some pharmaceutical companies into a nosedive. To be sure, some of this news has only a short-term impact on companies (particularly when it's *perception* about a bill versus actual *passage* of the bill), and eventually, bottom-line issues about the company and market will probably win out, but you should be vigilant about the news on regulations and its impact.

One reason I'll discuss in more detail in Trend Tip 9 is that sometimes when a major company takes a dive, it can be worth snapping it up at a discount, for that company may well rebound fairly quickly. The beauty, and aggravation, of politics is its cyclical nature. What if the Democrats do allow for negotiation on drug prices? In a few years, we might see the Republicans lifting the controls. Either way we aren't likely to see the stability of a major pharmaceutical like Johnson & Johnson waver. This is a key way in which doing your homework comes in handy.

You can distinguish between short-term hits and a real nosedive by looking at the company's fundamental financials, as always, relative to its competitors. Is the company well-positioned to recover from these regulatory hits (and has the stock done so in the past in other similar situations)? Does it have the cash or financing on the balance sheet to support new initiatives that can make up for this regulatory hit? Are there other products or businesses that seem ready to compensate for this loss? By predicting the trend—up or down—you have a better chance of determining when the stock may fall for the short term, and you might buy it as a bargain.

The Weatherman Can Make You Rich

At the time of writing this book, we've just emerged from hurricane season with nary a scratch. Thank goodness. What's more, the previous spring's long-term forecast had predicted it was going to be an enormous hurricane year. People stocked up on supplies, mapped out escape routes—some even relocated, frightened of another Hurricane Katrina.

What happened trendwise? Well, let's think: lots of things. Who would be the most pleased that a hurricane did not wreak devastation on the United States, aside from the happy homeowners living in hurricane prone regions? Insurance companies, of course. Insurers of property saw their earnings soar. Shareholders of Allstate, one of the largest insurance companies in America, found their stock up 15 percent since pre-hurricane season. The opposite happened back in 2005, the year of the Katrina tragedy. That summer, the stock was trading above $60. An investor watching the weather forecasts would have known that an extremely volatile hurricane season was expected for late summer and early fall. If she had sold her shares then, she would have saved herself a pretty penny when Allstate's stock plunged into the low $50s in early September and didn't recover until the fall of 2006.

The lesson? Watch the weather with all the attentiveness of the weatherperson, and predict how it can drive trends and make you a buck. Weather forecasting has become increasingly reliable in recent years, making this type of trend spotting even more effective. Even small things you might not think about are driven by weather. Some of them are predictable. Think about winter: if snowfall is predicted to be heavy that year, you can count on companies like Compass Minerals, which makes and sells rock, evaporated, and solar salts for deicing highways and driveways, to have a spike in their stock in the fall. But don't forget the season! A lot of energy stocks are cyclical with seasonal weather, since a cold winter means more use of heating oil and a hot summer means more electricity for air conditioning.

I bought Compass Minerals stock in the late summer of 2004, when it was trading around $20, and sold it in February 2005, when it was at $25. I skipped it the next year, when we were expecting a warm winter, and then bought it again in the fall of 2006 when the stock was at $26, and I'm still holding it now, while it's near $35 in February, but I'll probably sell soon. I suppose I could have held it the whole time, but I managed to do other things with my money during those spring and summer months, and the tactic of buying in fall, selling in spring has worked well for me.

Oil, gas, and electricity prices are also driven by the weather forecast. As I write this book, crude-oil prices in the first quarter of 2007 are heading upward. This first quarter price rise trend has occurred for each of the preceding five years—in part because it's winter and heating season drives up the demand for oil. This winter has been unusually warm, though, so the rise in price must be attributed to something else. With oil, you have to keep in mind other factors in addition to the weather, such as oil supply.

As I'll stress in later chapters, supply and demand are the basis for the market. Trends have an impact on what people want, but sometimes what people want is in tight supply. This scenario creates a product or service that will command a high price. If the forecast predicts cold weather, and oil is in short supply, you'll find that oil prices will spike higher than predicted. If the forecast is for a warmer winter, but oil is in short supply, you'll find that prices will also increase—just probably not as severely as they would with colder weather. The world's supply of oil is reportedly on the decline, and inventory levels make a huge difference in price. If global supply is dwindling, even decreased demand due to a warm winter will not offset the increased price of oil.

If you combine the tip of watching the weather with the Six Degrees of Making Bacon, you can extrapolate weather pricing to companies beyond ExxonMobil or Shell. Take a company like Frontline, which operates tankers for shipping crude oil. If you owned stock in the company, you would definitely have wanted to anticipate the trend of warmer weather and the effect it would have on the stock. Frontline was riding high in late 2004, but three consecutive winters of above-average temperatures decreased the demand for heating oil. Not surprisingly, the stock has declined steadily since then, dipping into the low $30s by the spring of 2006. It did see a jump of nearly 50 percent during that summer, corresponding to a record high price for a barrel of oil, but was back down to the low $30s by January as another warm winter took its toll.

Frontline does offer a terrific dividend, however, which makes it easier to ride out these ups and downs, and insulates the stock somewhat from larger declines. When you're looking at companies that may be affected by unpredictable factors like weather, it's always better to find one that offers such a dividend, which can keep you from losing your shirt in case you do need to take a loss. Dividend-paying companies often prove to be stable stocks, since a dividend-paying history means that the company has a steady stream of profits from which to pay those dividends. So while this sometimes limits high growth in your investment, it can offer good protection against big losses.

Soothe Your Fears

There are so many things to worry about. The news can be scary, even if there is only a remote chance of the headlines' affecting you personally. That doesn't mean people don't prepare themselves anyway. I find myself pouring lots of my money into securing my family—from cars with the highest crash-test ratings to home security systems—even when I know my fears are most likely (hopefully!) unfounded. I know I'm not the only one by a long shot and, in such a way, trends are pushed along by scary news. As a result, there is money to be made. I call this soothing my fears by investing wisely.

What are you personally afraid of? Terrorist strikes? Environmental havoc? *Chances are, your greatest fear is also someone else's greatest fear. You might as well make yourself feel better by making a buck on it.* Maybe that means investing in Roche, the company that makes Tamiflu, one of only two drugs that can purportedly treat avian flu. The stock was trading around $100 until 2005, when the share price shot up dramatically due to scary news about how avian flu might become an epidemic. The price doubled within six months and has stayed near $200 ever since. This huge spike occurred despite any concrete evidence that the drug would actually help in the event of an outbreak—and despite any evidence that the flu had mutated to a point where it could infect humans on a massive scale. (You'd have to buy Roche on a foreign exchange, but it'd be worth it to have your money double in six months.)

But don't get too fancy here. You might think that, after 9/11 or Katrina, the stock prices of all the insurance companies would be going up because Americans are likely to be more worried in the aftermath of a costly tragedy, and might flock to buy insurance to protect themselves. But both those events cost the insurance companies billions of dollars, and many stopped even offering insurance in coastal regions that are most vulnerable to hurricane strikes. To be sure, people will spend money to safeguard themselves, their families, and their property. But you have to weigh the larger set of factors that will either help or hurt the companies' bottom lines; nobody, especially not an insurance company, wants to leave themselves open to billions of dollars in losses. Companies respond to major events that impact their financials, so after taking hits from 9/11 and Katrina claims, the insurance companies are being more careful (in the near term) to avoid vulnerable areas for fear of those situations recurring. So it's often better to look for companies that benefit from soothing our fears rather than the ones that may suffer if those same fears come true.

Cyclical Industries Are Important

Watch the economy and heed the warning signs for particular cyclical industries. When pocketbooks are squeezed, what is the first thing to go? Certain luxury goods, vacations, and dining out certainly are all on the list. Likewise, when people have cash to burn, where might they spend it? Perhaps in high-end retail, second homes, house improvements, or entertainment. Scour the news for signs of an improving economy (high economic growth rate, low unemployment) that signal a willingness by consumers to spend. Conversely, when consumer debt levels are high and there's uncertainty about job security, it usually signals the end of the successful retail cycle.

As I pointed out in the Trend Tip 2 chapter, a good example of something to keep an eye on is interest rates. The level at which the Federal Reserve Bank sets rates has a huge impact on the direction of savings, the housing market, and the high-end-goods market, to name just a few. Another factor to keep your news junkie eye on is oil prices. As oil prices trend up or down, they impact the economy in many ways as industries reliant on oil, like airlines, as well as the individual consumer's spending power are affected.

Look for What the Influentials Are Doing

By following the news closely, you can also find the names of specific people you can pay attention to—those investors who somehow manage to make things work time after time. I certainly believe in luck, but some people consistently do so well that you can put a certain amount of faith in them and follow their lead.

Warren Buffett is probably the king of investors, and everyone knows about him, his influence, and his financial genius. There are also lesser known people like Sam Zell. He started out buying real estate from financially distressed owners in 1968, and by 1986 he was on the *Forbes* list of the richest 400 people in America, with $200 million. Now he's worth more than $4 billion. Zell invests by looking for industries that he thinks have a future, then learning everything he can about them. So if you follow his lead, you're following a man who is deeply savvy and deeply informed, and as sure a bet as you're going to find in the market. Maybe even set a Google Alert in his name, in addition to keeping track of what he is doing through paying attention to the financial media.

I'm particularly impressed with what Sam Zell did with American Commercial Lines, a company that manufactures and operates barges. Zell did his homework and found there had been a barge-building spree in 1979. He knew that the average life of a barge was 25 years, and so he expected another surge in demand in 2004. Visionary that he is, Zell bought some of the company's bonds in 2002. These bonds represented the company's debt, and because American Commercial Lines was in serious debt at the time, Zell thought it likely that the company would go bankrupt. In a bankruptcy, the stock becomes virtually worthless, and the bondholders end up in a much better position. Sure enough, the company was forced into bankruptcy in 2003, but it went public two years later and the stock soared, tripling in around eighteen months. Now this is clearly a big-wave-surfer strategy and should be attempted only by the savviest of investors, but this is just an example of the type of business a smart investor like Sam Zell looks for. Zell is also involved in the waste-collection, communications, home building, and other industries, so you can even diversify your portfolio as you play Follow the Leader.

Watch the Super Bowl . . . for Its Ads

Beginning as early as when I was a five-year-old, selling those sunglasses at the Jersey Shore, I've seen the value in marketing products properly. Back then, I'd buy the sunglasses wholesale in bulk from my beloved grandma, a formidable immigrant who couldn't read or write but who had the savvy to own her own small grocery store. After picking up my inventory for the day, I'd head to the busiest, sunniest part of the beach.

But what I quickly noticed was that the quality and nature of the product were not the most important factors in selling it. Even at age five, I could see clearly that the cotton candy booth down the beach was always packed. Clouds of whipped sugar made for an extravaganza of color and a sweet aroma. Once a few people came to the booth to take a look, others would notice, head over to check it out, and wind up buying pink spun sugar themselves. But the nearby ice tea stand, despite serving delicious tea, was always fairly sleepy—tea just wasn't as exciting despite being cold and refreshing on a hot day. So I quickly adjusted my methods. I found a colorful cardboard display for my glasses, and whenever I got a customer who wanted to purchase a pair I would take my sweet old time making change. The longer they stuck around my product, the more likely I would get more customers to take notice and head over to check out and buy my wares.

Of course, a lot has changed from my young days hawking sunglasses. But my early experiences taught me that making money is largely about how a product gets placed in the market. You have to spend creative energy, time, and money in order to make money. For this reason, I've always kept my eye on Madison Avenue. What are the advertisers hyping and how, and who is spending money on getting their brand name out there in a clever, effective way? Usually companies with large marketing budgets are companies to keep your eye on.

The way I look at it, if you saw an ad, it is likely that someone else did, too. Ad money translates into exposure and into sales. Where and what are companies heavily promoting? Is it sleeping pills? A restaurant chain? Maybe a new beer?

In 2004, television viewers and radio listeners started seeing a wave of smart new ads from NutriSystem, a company that makes diet foods (not to be confused with Nutraceutical, the company I mentioned earlier, which makes nutritional supplements). NutriSystem had been relying on a tired old campaign featuring Zora Andrich, the bachelorette who won "Joe Millionaire" back in 2003. The ads weren't working anymore, and in late 2004 a new marketing director, Tom Connerty, took over and started a new campaign that was contemporary and dynamic.

I noticed these ads in early 2005 and was struck by how NutriSystem suddenly seemed much more attractive. When I looked into the company, I found it had had a rough history, including a bankruptcy in 1993. But in 2002 it had been taken over by an investor group that seemed to have the right credentials (industry experience, track record) to be able to turn this company around, though the results through 2004 were still pretty discouraging. I also knew that Americans were getting heavier and heavier, and that there would be a growing demand for diet systems. And I liked NutriSystem's subscription model—they send you food, and you lose weight by eating only their products—which requires customers to stick with their product for a while in order to see results. So I felt all the demand would be there if they could just improve their appeal.

Then I heard that NutriSystem would be filing its results for the first quarter of 2005 in May. I started hearing positive expectations, and then they announced their revenues were five times higher than in the previous quarter, and three times higher than in the best quarter of 2004. I bought the stock at $11, and happily watched as the company continued to improve its marketing. By January 2006, the stock was at $40, and four months later, a year to the day after my purchase, it was at $65.

I decided to celebrate my anniversary with NutriSystem by dumping the company. The ads were still good, including very handsome new shots of the food they sell, which looked so good I almost ordered some—even though I wasn't on a diet! But I wasn't sure the growth was going to be sustained once the novelty of the "new NutriSystem" wore off. I thought the company would continue to do well, but that the rapid growth would settle down and the stock would plateau. After all, marketing can get you only so far and can't keep a company afloat on its own. I missed some of the upside, as the company reached as high as $76 very shortly after I sold, but I thought a gain of nearly 600 percent was enough, thank you very much!

When you do invest in a company because of its marketing, you must—as always—do the research to make sure the company is actually solid, the way I did with NutriSystem. As we all know, advertising is a powerful force these days, and it's easy to get snookered by a bit of flash that proves to be smoke and mirrors.

Surrounding yourself with news and keeping your ears open at all times, is one of the best ways to be turned on to trends. Whether political, fashion, health, regulatory, science, or sports, all types of news tell us about trends in the making, and can be turned into a buck.

TREND TIP 6

Study the Stats

How Pictures Tell a Thousand Words

I know, I know—Statistics: yuck! But before you skip over Trend Tip 6, I want to assure you that this kind of stat watching is fun—and easy. It has nothing to do with number crunching. You don't need sophisticated knowledge, an Excel program, or a graphing calculator. I promise. You just need to do a little research, and to use Trend Tip 5, Be a News Junkie. You should also combine this tip with the Six Degrees of Making Bacon game. Even a cursory examination of certain data will enable you to predict trends being set in all directions.

Some financial experts do nothing but study charts. While there is a real science to interpreting charts, you don't need a math degree to understand how certain numbers reflect certain trends. Whether it is the rise in population creating a future energy shortage, the global warming trend leading to a need for pollutant-reducing technologies, or the increase in obesity causing certain diet programs to soar, watching how the numbers are trending will help you determine which wave to ride and for how long.

It's All Demographics, Demographics, Demographics

One of the easiest and most effective ways to spy trends is to follow population studies. Keep an eye on the statistics. Who is getting older, who is getting fatter, who is getting sicker? Where are people being born? Who's making the big bucks, and at what age? Where are they spending their money, and where are they choosing to live? The list goes on and on. Out of each statistic, there are many ways you can anticipate how trends might arise and, from this, how you might find companies to invest in and profit from. Where do you find stats like this? Lots of places. Almanacs, the web, Google searches, TV and radio news, government organizations, nonprofits, pollsters, magazines and newspapers (see Appendix A for some examples). Every day I seem to read a new statistic.

The ways in which populations shift around affect every

part of our world—and our economy. Let's take current demographic shifts as an example. Experts predict that by 2010 a perfect storm of factors will come together. Birth rates in the United States are dropping, the baby boomers will begin retiring, and business will be growing. As a result, we will have fewer workers but more jobs. Some readers may doubt that the boomers will really be retiring, given all the press about how people aren't saving enough for retirement and will have to work longer. But I'm confident that plenty of boomers, workaholics though they are, will have had it with working. If possible, they will want to cash in on their 401(k)s and have time to do all the things they missed out on while working so hard in their twenties, thirties, forties, and fifties. For those who can't afford to retire fully, or who get restless when they have excess leisure time, they'll likely work schedules that give them flexibility, whether in part-time jobs or by freelancing. So, we will likely face a labor shortage, which means that businesses are going to have to fight for the talent pool.

What does this mean for investors? With the predicted labor shortage and traditional head-hunting fees being significant, one can recognize the upside potential of an online employment company like Monster.com. This is one of my favorite businesses. A company like Monster is poised to benefit from a labor shortage. I missed the initial boom in this stock, back when it went public in the late 1990s, mostly because I was worried about an overheated stock market and potential recession, and I feared the job market might tighten for a while. I could have bought at about $10 and would have enjoyed a tenfold increase a year later. This is a good example of the wisdom of not allowing one missed opportunity to sour you on a stock and that there can be good reason to buy it at some later date. I ended up making an excellent return on my money on this one in the end. When the stock fell to $7.00 in 2003 and the economy was bouncing back, I finally bought Monster and have enjoyed a healthy gain of more than 500 percent from studying my stats back in 2002 and early 2003.

At the time, there was a great deal of press about the dismal employment situation, as the U.S. economy wasn't generating nearly as many jobs as it had been in the 1990s. This, of course, became a central argument in John Kerry's unsuccessful presidential campaign in 2004. It's no surprise that investors were pulling out of Monster in 2001 and 2002, sending the stock price down from about $60 to below $15 (and eventually below $10) in a little over a year. My response to this drop, and to a little bit of research, was to realize that an opportunity was emerging.

For one thing, Monster's revenues had actually remained strong in 2002, suggesting it could weather a tough employment situation for a while. I felt the huge tax cuts of 2001 would jump-start the economy soon, and that Monster's services would soon be in demand again. So I looked into the statistics a little more, and realized that many of the financial companies were starting to regain their confidence in the economy and to invest again in new companies, particularly in new technology companies that constituted what would come to be known as Web 2.0. Plus, the hedge funds were doing extremely well and private equity was heating up. This suggested to me that there would soon be demand for the kind of technology and financial jobs that Monster is especially strong in filling.

I bought the stock at $10 in February 2003 and waited for other investors to catch up. Sure enough, after dipping a bit further and making me wish I'd waited longer, Monster's stock started to rise in a few months, and it got just below $29 before the end of 2003. By January 2006 it was at $47. I missed my chance to sell then, before the stock dipped to $40, because I was still bullish on the company's prospects. After a few more months, the stock climbed back up to $50 at the beginning of 2007, and I decided to sell when I started to see statistics suggesting the economy might be cooling off a bit. I could have made more, but I ended up with a 40 percent profit in just three years, not too shabby.

One of my favorite ways to get news about demographics shifts is listening to the radio. I love the radio, and always have something on in the background, whether it is the Doug Stephan show (on which I'm a regular commentator) or NPR. Sometimes I'm a serial channel flipper. In the car, I press Scan endlessly, no doubt driving my companions crazy. That was how I got onto one of the trends I recently capitalized on. In the spring of 2003, I couldn't help but notice how many Spanish-language radio stations were on the dial. As I was flipping, it seemed like nearly every other channel was in Spanish. I'm nearly fluent in Spanish, so it's fun—and good practice—for me to listen in. I realized the boom in Spanish radio was in response to the rapidly growing Hispanic population in the United States—one whose buying power I think has been undervalued by investors.

In March 2003, I looked up stocks of leading Spanish-language media companies and found that Spanish Broadcasting Systems was a $6.00 stock that had been as high as $42 during the inflationary dot-com days of 2000. Radio stocks in general were depressed at that time—yet this was a niche that I could not deny was growing. I bought SBSA at $6 a share. Then, in April 2004, I sold for more than $10, because I had learned that competitors were entering the market—the same reason I sold Univision for such a profit in 2001. SBSA was close to a double for me.

This is but one of millions of examples about how population shifts can help predict trends and help grow your bank account. The following are some other types of statistics that I use for guides in investing.

Mother Earth's Numbers

To look for such shifts, another great method is to the environmental stats—storm trends, climate changes, dwindling resources. They can tell you a lot about potential trends.

As I've said earlier, I've been tracking green companies for some time now. While the issues affecting us are myriad, there is no question that the environment on the whole, in one way or another, is going to be a driving force of trends in the next century. The stats on this are solid, and the rising oil prices are further evidence of a need for alternative and renewable energy sources. The questions are, how, where, and in what ways can we invest wisely in green technologies?

In April 2006, I bought Covanta, a waste-disposal and energy-production company based in Fairfield, New Jersey. It's another Sam Zell company; he's the brilliant investor I mentioned as a guide, and I followed him on this buy, to the great benefit of my portfolio. Zell was interested in the developing business of turning waste into energy—a green process that uses new technologies to diminish landfill space and generate energy with fewer greenhouse gases. He did his research and realized that cities pay people to take away garbage! The excess garbage that can't be used is stored in landfills, which Covanta owns and operates. (Covanta is also involved in independent power production, water treatment, waste transfer, and other services.) Covanta acquired ARC, a waste-to-energy company, and combined their operations; this meant increased revenues and profits due to economies of scale. Not surprisingly, Covanta has been a real winner; when I bought in April 2006, I paid $16 a share, and at the time of this writing it's above $22 after climbing above $24. I'll continue to hold this one; it's green and it's Zell, and I can't imagine a better combination.

Often you can combine several statistics to hit upon a trend. Look at Arizona and its population growth. It is booming. But also look at natural resources, and you will see statistic after statistic about the drought in Arizona and the water crisis. What does this mean for a trend watcher? More people + less water = higher demand for water. There is the trend. Where is a company that can profit from this trend? The company that owns the water, for starters. A perfect example is a company called Pico Holdings, which through its subsidiary, Vidler Water Company, is buying up water rights in the southwestern United States. It will then sell or lease water sources to private and public users. It's a smart strategy in a part of the country where the price of water is certainly only going to increase in upcoming years. This example shows that you can combine demographic statistics in powerful ways to yield interesting trends and companies that stand to profit from these trends.

Supply and Demand Never Goes Out of Style

As I've said before, the stock market is based on this concept, and it's not rocket science. But we sometimes ignore the obvious things in life. One good trend-spotting technique is to look for the numbers of products and services that are needed versus what is available. You don't necessarily need to get data at the most granular level; top-level statistics about overall supply and demand are usually sufficient. Take copper as an example. Copper is an essential part of new construction, as it's needed for piping and wiring. In the early 2000s, when the American economy started warming up again and the Asian economies continued to surprise with their growth, copper supplies went down, demand stayed high, and the price rose. Eventually things got so crazy that thieves were stealing copper gutters off their neighbors' homes to take advantage of the high price. I know someone who actually painted his beautiful copper gutters brown, just to hide the fact that they were copper! But then copper production surged to meet the demand, and this sent prices down again. It may be common sense, but a lot of people made and lost fortunes on the price of copper.

Of course, copper is a commodity, and most average investors should avoid the commodity markets because they're complicated and unreliable. There are ways to apply this type of thinking to the stock market, too, though. For one thing, if you'd noticed the housing market warming up in late 2002, you might have bought stocks like Encore or Freeport McMoRan, which were trading around $5 and $10, respectively. These companies in early 2006 were worth nearly $50 and $70, respectively—more than a tenfold increase on your investment! In this case, you would have noticed the demand for copper growing, but instead of risking your hard-earned money in the crazy commodities market, you could have looked to a company that makes its living by knowing the copper markets, and by investing in them made yourself a nice bundle in three years.

During this time period you could have applied the same logic at the same time to aluminum, another necessary component of construction. If you'd looked into aluminum along with copper in late 2002, you might have found a company called the Aluminum Corporation of China, which was poised to take advantage of the booming Chinese economy. This stock was trading around $2 at the time, and the past few years have seen the stock climb almost to $30, while paying a very nice 5 percent dividend yield. A similar line of thinking would have been an investment in Alcoa, which was below $20 in late 2002 and shot up to $40 by the end of 2003.

You can also apply the Six Degrees of Making Bacon to trends spotted by monitoring supply and demand. For example, with demand for oil rising in 2006, oil companies had to do more drilling to keep supplies flowing. Some investors would read news about oil demand, and invest in ExxonMobil. But other opportunities are out there. In early 2006, I learned of a company called Maverick Tube, which manufactured equipment used in the exploration and production of oil—things like tubing and joint couplings. This stock was in the low $50s when I recommended it in May 2006. Five months later the company was acquired by Tenaris, another pipeline company, for $65 a share. A 25 percent gain isn't bad for five months!

But be careful in using this technique, because supply and demand can cut both ways. For a lesson about how the laws of supply and demand can hurt your portfolio, you can look at a company like Vonage. When this company was started in 2000, it got great buzz. Like Skype, it offered a way to use the internet to supply cheaper phone service with all kinds of neat possibilities, like linking your phone to your email account. The technology was rough in the beginning, with echoes and delays, but many people still felt there was real potential. Vonage ultimately went public in May 2006 at a price of $17. By then, the company had moved from being a new, niche technology to being a mainstream company that many people beyond the technophiles were using. Yet the stock dropped immediately after the IPO and, as of this writing, hasn't even come close to recovering. It's a possible acquisition candidate for its customer base, but never for the same share price investors paid for it in the beginning.

So what happened? Demand was steadily increasing for internet phone, and many people think it's the way all phone calls will be made in the future. Skype never went to IPO, but many thought it would have performed much better. The problem was that while demand for internet phone was rising, allowing Vonage to add more customers, the supply also rose significantly. That is, by 2006, Vonage had far too much competition from other internet telephone services. Traditional phone companies like Verizon quickly offered their own plans, as did cable companies like Time Warner. Then there were many other, smaller internet phone companies offering their own inexpensive plans, often as low as $19.95 per month. It's not that Vonage necessarily did anything wrong; they just succumbed to the laws of supply and demand, and their cost structure and technology didn't support the lower price as well as offerings by competitors.

The same thing happened with TiVo. Everyone was

talking about this company in the late '90s—here was a new technology that allowed people to watch television shows at the time they wanted—and without having to suffer through all those tiresome ads that seem to be repeated at least five times every hour these days. TiVo seemed set to revolutionize the television industry, and to make a fortune in the process. The stock certainly did well at first, opening at $16 in September 1999 and rising quickly to $40. But then the cable companies started offering their own versions of TiVo. Once again, for TiVo, supply outpaced demand. The stock started to decline in early 2000, and it really sank in late 2000, when it dipped below $5 at the end of December. It has yet to bounce back.

As an investor, when you see a company offering the same service as countless others, you should do your research and make sure you're paying attention to the stats about supply and demand, and look before you leap. Of course this isn't always predictable—many an analyst was bullish on TiVo at the time of its IPO. If you bought a stock like TiVo, don't blame yourself for not predicting the future. But make sure you pay attention to these essential issues of supply and demand; nothing is ever static, especially in the financial markets and in technology, and you have to be able to adapt to save your profits or cut your losses. So I'll stress again the importance of comparing a company with its competitors. How it performs against current (and potential) competitors can tell you if the company is poised to capitalize on the supply-and-demand trend you noticed or get hammered by it.

Follow Your Tax Dollar

Study the government's yearly budget. If the feds are planning to spend more on the military, for instance, you can count on growth in certain companies in that sector. Earlier in this book, for example, I mentioned Halliburton. Everyone knew that we were gearing up for war in early 2003, and it was a no-brainer that military budgets would be increasing, especially for the kinds of services provided by a contractor like Halliburton. Very few companies have the ability to operate in a war zone, and there was never any question that they'd be receiving a large number of contracts. (Despite the charges leveled by many activists, this would have happened regardless of whether the former CEO was the sitting vice president.) Not surprisingly, the stock has done extremely well over the past few years, quadrupling in price even despite headlines about overcharging.

Another company that has benefited from the war in Iraq is Northrop Grumman, an aerospace and electronics company that services the U.S. military. If you'd bought this stock in early 2003, you would have paid $40. Four years later, the company is worth more than $70, and it offers a small dividend to garnish those capital gains.

But it's not just the military that's affected by governmental budgetary allocations. Take education, for example. When George W. Bush signed the No Child Left Behind Act into law in early 2002, schools had to scramble to purchase new materials to satisfy the new curriculum and testing standards being set in place because of the new law. These new materials aren't created by the government—they're created by publishers who sell textbooks and other educational materials. No Child Left Behind meant there would be enormous demand for these publishers' products. So who are the big educational publishers? McGraw-Hill is one of the three biggest. Anyone prescient enough to foresee this trend could have bought this stock at $30, or even less, in 2002 or early 2003. This clever investor would now be sitting on an investment worth more than twice as much as he or she put down, as the stock has climbed steadily since early 2003 and as of this writing is up to nearly $70.

You can learn about budgetary plans in the newspapers, of course. As I've said before, all the trend-watching tips in this book can be used in conjunction with one another; here think Trend Tip 5, Be a News Junkie. But another place to learn about government budget plans is to watch the State of the Union address. You'll have to suffer through the usual politician's exaggerations, and those interminable standing ovations, and in fact you may want to just read the transcript in the next day's newspaper. However you decide to deal with the SOTU (as they call it in Washington), you can find useful information about how the government plans to spend its money in the coming year.

In the 2007 SOTU, for example, George W. Bush promised to fund alternative energy sources at a higher level. This kind of funding—if approved, of course—could boost the profits of companies that produce hydrogen fuel cells or ethanol. Now, you probably don't want to rush out and buy a company like Ballard, which makes fuel cells, or Earth BioFuels, which is Willie Nelson's alternative-fuel company, just because of a promise from a politician. But you might well want to file the information away for future reference, and keep your eye out for other news that suggests an increasing demand for this type of technology. It's worth mentioning that this type of technology is very tricky. Sometimes it moves faster than expected; sometimes slower. As I mentioned before, venture capitalists are smart at figuring out the technology trend curve, so it's very helpful to watch their moves.

The Health of the Nation

The stats about health reveal a wealth of trend information: from the size of our aging population, to obesity, to numbers involving smokers, to stats about the myriad of cancers and other ills, to types of drugs used by whom and for what. Do an internet search for the National Center for Health Statistics to get up-to-date information from the Centers for Disease Control and Prevention (at the time of this writing, the site is at http://www.cdc.gov/nchs/). Each of these statistics can be used to determine trends and capitalize on them.

The most obvious trend to dissect is that of baby boomers aging, which I've mentioned before. This enormous population presents a sector with a huge number of health needs—not to mention financial resources to pay for those needs. My own parents aren't boomers, but they are active seniors and, no matter how healthy they remain, they still have issues cropping up. Our bodies unfortunately do this over time. Like so many others, my parents and their siblings and friends will need joints replaced, operations for broken hips, and all kinds of medical services.

When you extrapolate this insight to the baby boom generation, many of whom have spent decades jogging and working out and putting unprecedented stresses on their bodies, you can anticipate that there will be a huge demand for new knees and hips. How does this simple trend translate into cash? Do your research and find well-managed companies that will capitalize on this trend. Take Zimmer Holdings, for instance. A friend turned me on to Zimmer, an innovator in orthopedics that specializes in minimally invasive hip replacements and knee devices. As everyone knows, an elderly person who falls and breaks a hip is often in serious trouble—not because of the injury itself but because of the complications that can arise from operating on an aging body. Zimmer's less invasive approach is perfect for our aging population, and I was confident this company was going to make a lot of money in the coming years. After doing some research, I wrote an AOL blog entry in March 2006 saying that it was a good value in the $70s, so when it dropped to $65 in late April, I grabbed it. As it turned out, the stock kept dropping and sank almost down to $50 in the summer of 2006. But I didn't panic, as I knew the company had serious long-term potential.

Sure enough, the stock started climbing, and it is now

above $80. I could sell now and take a gain of more than 20 percent, but with the aging boomers likely to keep driving up demand, I'm going to hold this one for a while. If you were smarter and more prescient than I am, you might have come to this realization back in January 2003, when the company was trading at $40, and you would have doubled your money!

You can also look at other health statistics, then apply the Six Degrees of Making Bacon method. Let's look at the growing obesity problem in America—and abroad in Europe and Asia, for that matter. At the time of this book's publication and according to the National Center for Health Statistics, more than 60 percent of the U.S. population is obese, and this number is on the rise. It is a sad statistic, but what does it tell you? Using the Six Degrees concept, we can spot trends in many directions. There may be trends involving diet foods, fad diets, antiobesity medication, tummy staples, even plus-size clothing. Taking it another step, the rise in obesity translates into a rise in diabetes, which translates into kidney problems. What is bad news for the diabetic is good news for the nephrologists and kidney-drug makers who have gotten rich off the problem. But it also will drive drug makers to find a cure for diabetes, and you should keep your eyes peeled for news stories involving breakthroughs on that front as well. This one statistic regarding the growing obesity epidemic can help you make money in a variety of market sectors.

Let's focus on one of these sectors. As we know from Trend Tip 3, ours is a vain culture. Couple this with the obesity problem, and you have a significant group of people who will be seeking to lose weight. Now do your research. What diet programs out there are effective? Talk to people you know who are trying to lose weight; ask the neighbors who have lost weight how they did it. Although I discovered NutriSystem because of its advertising push, I could just as likely have heard about it from friends who were on the plan and were finding it successful. If I'd heard about this company from a few friends at cocktail parties back in 2003 or 2004, I would still have made a huge profit on it, just as I did earlier from watching its ads and keeping tabs on its revenues.

There is no end to the number of trends that you can dig up by studying the stats. Be a detective, dig deep, play the Six Degrees game, and always remember human behavior. You will be able to turn a statistic into a way to make money, and probably have a lot of fun in the process.

TREND TIP 7

The World Is Your Oyster

Look Beyond Your Borders

In our increasingly globalized world, trends can start anywhere. Unless you've been in a cave for the last year, it's no surprise that looking to places like China and India might be a good idea. Do your research on areas in the globe where natural resources or human capital may be of value. But be smart about it—sociopolitical instability can be the ruin of your investment.

For example, the sheer population size of China, combined with its new embrace of capitalism, presents a vast platform on which business will thrive. The growing number of consumers in China likely means autos and credit cards are going to be big businesses there in the next decade. Think of other things—from health care to gambling to expanding diets—and you get a huge picture of profit arenas.

I have mentioned before what a big effect the aging population will have on the work force. There aren't enough people being born to replace those who are retiring. As the economy grows in this country, and more and more jobs are created, there are going to be fewer talented people of working age to fill those jobs. Who is going to fill the void? Certainly, as I've commented before, companies like Monster.com and Hotjobs.com are going to benefit, and skilled laborers are going to find themselves in higher and higher demand. But outsourcing is also going to grow; it's already at a significant level, and it will only increase to fill the jobs being vacated by retiring baby boomers.

Provided you are doing careful research, investing in foreign countries has great potential. That said, there are many factors to weigh in the equation, and even if you have a joint degree in political economics and international relations, tread cautiously. These are some key tips to keep in mind.

Eye Emerging Markets

What was a no-go zone yesterday is open to dollars today. Emerging markets yield new consumer bases, natural resources, and intellectual capital. From Russia to Libya to

South Africa, in the last decades we've witnessed many countries step in line with global capitalism. Where is the next big place? Cuba? What about the Latin American and African countries that have great natural resources and are flirting with democracy and political stability? And what about those countries, like Thailand, who on paper seem in lockstep with capitalism, but may be trending toward anti-growth policies? Look carefully. Are they really a safe bet?

In August 2005 I attended the World Summit on Sustainable Development in Johannesburg. This annual conference is a United Nations get-together where global players convene to address important economic and environmental issues from around the planet. Thousands of delegates negotiated about everything from reducing carbon dioxide emissions to policies for AIDS prevention to promoting Third World exports. The central players, of course, were the world's governments. In addition, a host of nongovernmental organizations (NGOs)—everybody from Greenpeace to the World Conservation Union to the Ford Foundation to the Jewish National Fund—were present and quite vocally accounted for. Finally, Big Business was there to defend against its critics and at the same time promote its ideas on profitable, sustainable development. These companies recognized the crucial need to be a part of planetary problem-solving and at the same time seize an opportunity to show off their good works to the world.

The most compelling story here, however, was that of South Africa's little-known economic boom, which crept up on the world with few investors noticing. In the 1970s and

1980s, South Africa became an international pariah, as its loathsome apartheid system of racial discrimination and categorization became the object of boycotts and corporate-divestiture campaigns. Apartheid came to an end in 1990, and the world celebrated Nelson Mandela's release from prison. Investors were nervous at the time, as the future direction of the country hung in the balance. When Mandela was elected South Africa's president in 1994, he offered a conciliatory message of leadership to the multiracial nation and brought a new feeling of calm and optimism to the business community. Indeed, for many, South Africa came to symbolize global hope for Third World development, economic as well as political.

That's one reason why this revitalized nation received the honor of hosting the World Summit. But investors still hung back, imposing what might be called a "country-risk discount" on the economy here. Moreover, starting in the late '90s, a series of international economic shocks—in Russia, East Asia, and Latin America—rocked the world economy, and South Africa was not spared the jolt of these destabilizing tremors. The country's stock market and currency—the two best indicators of any nation's investment climate—both took hard hits, and nearly five years later, South Africa still found itself undervalued as the country tried to regain its footing.

But by 2005 things were turning around as South Africa recovered from the problems of the late 1990s and its economy started warming up. The South African company I liked best was SABMiller (which is traded on foreign exchanges). Most folks haven't heard of SABMiller, which was formerly known as South African Breweries before acquiring Miller Brewing Company, but it's been around for more than a century and is the world's second-largest brewer, with annual beer volumes in excess of 20 million hectoliters. SABMiller is also the world's largest bottler and distributor of Coca-Cola products outside the United States.

SABMiller's impact is both local and global. It has an astounding 98 percent share of South Africa's beer market. As I personally witnessed, the company's Castle Lager is the national brand of choice. SABMiller sponsors the national soccer team, the Bafani Bafani (Boys Boys), which has become a symbol of postapartheid patriotic unity. That's a level of brand equity and loyalty that few companies anywhere, in any industry, can match.

In July 2002, SAB completed its $5.4 billion acquisition of Miller, the second-largest brewer in the United States. The acquisition was a bold stroke for this South African company, and it spoke to the brewer's international potential. Since then the company has continued to acquire foreign brewers. To be sure, many good companies have hurt themselves through overacquisitiveness, but I believe SAB is different.

A full discussion about merger strategies is beyond the scope of this book but generally speaking, mergers tend to be successful when the strategy is well defined (cost cutting in overlapping business, expansion to new geographic regions, cross selling of products across distribution channels). And how realistic is it to achieve the merger cost savings or benefits touted as the rationale behind the merger? Track record is important as well: is it a company, like Citigroup, that has had a history of successfully integrating merged companies?

To me, the main benefit in SABMiller's merger lies in the firm's balanced geographic strategy, in which it seeks huge cash flow from big but mature markets, such as the United States, and reinvests that cash throw-off in fast-growing new markets, such as China. In fact, it's the second-largest and most profitable brewer in China, a huge beer-consuming country, with 27 breweries and a combined capacity of more than 31 million hectoliters.

In addition, SAB is a big player in many underserved markets; in fact, in partnership with local *cervecerias* (breweries) in El Salvador and Honduras, SAB controls 100 percent of those markets. Such local mergers are an astute strategy because brewing is a capital-intensive, volume-driven business; it is difficult for new or smaller brands to compete in a serious way. This allows a larger corporation to dominate the market more easily, and to make sure its investments in advertising and distribution achieve maximal profits.

Crucial to this point, the world market underestimates South African companies as well as South Africa, where so many people are so poor. Therefore, investors can get in cheap, benefiting from the aforementioned "country risk discount." Even so, investing in foreign companies is tricky, and it's worth explaining in detail. If you're willing to take the time to look for companies like SABMiller, with vision and international reach, and you're very careful to make sure its fundamentals are strong, as you would with any company, you may find yourself making quite a bit of money after buying at a discount.

This example also brings up another point: it is logistically more difficult to invest in foreign companies that don't yet trade in U.S. markets. The average investor might want to wait for an exciting foreign company to be offered in U.S. markets before investing. You'll read an example of this below.

Much of what you need to evaluate the foreign markets can be found, as usual, simply by reading your news sources. All the answers and great future home run stocks are there for the taking—just read between the lines and focus on stringing two and three themes together. What do I mean by stringing together a few themes? I knew that 2006 was going to be another year in which China would be "hot." The financial magazines wrote about the prospects. All the year-end predictions in the personal finance monthlies had experts pointing east. But I also saw that China had passed a law requiring a twofold increase in the use of alternative energy by 2020. I put these two themes together and bought Suntech Power (STP), a Chinese solar company that had recently "IPO'd" on the U.S. market.

I did my research and found Suntech's revenues and margins had been improving, and also found that it was talented at publicizing the company's accomplishments. Investor relations skillfulness is an important component of a stock's success. After all, if investors aren't aware of how well the company is doing, they won't be willing to pay up for those benefits—which speaks to what I mentioned before about investor *perception*. My January 2006 investment in Suntech was priced at $27.80 and turned into $37.90 when I sold at the end of April 2006. At that point, it seemed like the stock price had already built in much of the growth that could be expected of the company in the near term (meaning that the P/E was getting to be much higher than that of other renewable energy companies, to say nothing of energy companies overall). I missed the very top price of $42, and I bought higher than I could have by more than $5.00, but it doesn't matter because I still made money and didn't get greedy. If I had held on and waited for another peak, then I would have been sitting on a $23 stock only six weeks later.

Geopolitics Matters

In the late 1990s, Argentina's vast natural resources made the country look like a sure bet. Some people poured their life savings into Argentine bonds, but they weren't taking into account the shaky political situation. Suddenly the country went bankrupt, saw six different presidents in two years, and defaulted on all the money it owed to investors, leaving individuals worldwide with huge losses. A smart global investment takes into account not just the obvious value of the area but also the area's political stability—or instability, as the case may be.

I've discussed China many times. This is a 1.3 billion–person market, and many businesses are clamoring to tap into these consumers. But investors must consider that there are serious risks to companies in doing so. Remember, unlike in the United States, where rules and regulations are in place to protect businesses, business owners, and employees, in China the government can pretty much do as it pleases. Copyright rules are not often respected or enforced. Competition is fierce. Let's take a quick look at the internet in China. Who would be more excited to get into this massive market than eBay, the online auction site? And yet, the company's push into China proved to be incredibly complicated.

In late 2006, eBay announced it would be closing its main website in China. Instead, a Chinese-based internet company, Tom Online, was taking over and running the site. Competition within the marketplace was unexpected and strong, with several rival online auction houses outperforming eBay. If you'd bought the stock expecting a significant jump from eBay's China venture, you would have been disappointed. I mentioned in previous chapters how much regulations matter, but in emerging markets, they matter even more. In a highly regulated (and nuanced) industry like China's internet/media industries, it's tough to bet on the foreign player.

Even Google, as dominant as it is in the western world, simply can't compete with local-grown Chinese internet search company Baidu.com. (Google was at least savvy enough to have invested in Baidu before that company's

IPO, so it did enjoy some financial benefit.) Knowing the geopolitics involved in each emerging-market country can help steer investors into the right companies and away from the wrong ones. (In China, local internet companies were the right companies while foreign internet companies were the wrong ones in which to invest.)

Doing the Right Thing Abroad

As our world has gotten smaller through travel and advances in technology, we have all become more conscious of the problems around us. If you're following Trend Tip 5 about paying attention to the news, likely you will find yourself a bit depressed now and then: there is no question that the news can be a downer. The news media tend to paint an overall portrait of a world full of strife, despair, and challenges. How the public responds to this awareness, this knowledge of the suffering of others, is a force that sets trends in motion. One trend now is toward helping others. Whether it has to do with the rise of religion, or with the global war on terror, or with environmental catastrophes like the tsunami in Indonesia and the hurricane in New Orleans, people seem to be willing to do more to help. But as we've learned in Trend Tip 3, it's human nature to look out for oneself first. We like to spend money, and we like to spend it on ourselves, which is mixed with this increasing desire to spend it on others.

The result is a powerful new trend of people shopping

increasingly at companies that project an image of helping the world. Take Starbucks and its fair trade coffees, which Starbucks pledges to purchase at "fair" prices that protect coffee farmers from a drop in global coffee prices. As a consumer, I am willing to pay a premium for coffee grown by farmers in Uganda, Guatemala, Thailand, and many other places. As an investor, you can make money and feel good about it, since you're helping the disadvantaged enter the financial playing field. Online searches will give you many examples of publicly traded companies engaged in fair trade or in "moral trade" concepts, like Canadian diamonds versus the so-called African blood diamonds, an issue brought to public attention by the Leonardo di Caprio movie of the same name.

As I've said elsewhere in the book, it is important to be able to live with your investment decisions. It is all about personal comfort level. I personally advocate putting your money into causes and businesses that not only pay back—you make some money—but also give back so that your money is in part helping others. There is no more satisfying wave to ride, in my opinion, than making money while also helping make the world a better place.

Natural Resources Are Crucial

Everyone knows that the colonies founded by European powers provided essential natural resources to the colonizing countries: South America for Spain, North America for

Britain, and the Congo for Belgium. Though the colonial period is thankfully over, countries with strong natural resources can be excellent places to invest. You can put your money into the foreign companies operating in those resource-rich nations. But as I've stressed throughout this chapter, you need to be careful. At the risk of generalizing, I think many nations with excellent resources, especially oil, tend to be run by troublesome governments. The theory is that having natural resources to rely on makes it too easy for autocratic governments to make money off their oil, say, or their diamonds, which then frees them from having to invest in healthy economies. They can also seize this wealth for themselves, making stable political systems harder to achieve, which in turn hurts their economies. The examples are legion: Hugo Chavez in Venezuela, Sani Abacha in Nigeria, the Saudi government, and so on.

These rulers are often unafraid to nationalize their industries, seizing huge assets from foreign companies, thereby wiping out portions of your investment. Hugo Chavez in Venezuela and Evo Morales in Bolivia are the most prominent recent nationalizers. Autocratic rulers can interfere in other ways, too, as Russian president Vladimir Putin did in 2006 when he forced Royal Dutch Shell to give up half its stake in a $22 billion project on Sakhalin Island and sell it to Gazprom for a remarkably low price. It's a complicated story, and Shell didn't exactly handle itself well throughout the project, but Putin essentially muscled his way into the deal by using environmental objections to shake down Shell and claim its stake for Gazprom.

The issue started coming to a head in September 2006, when Putin canceled an environmental permit for Shell's project. This didn't have an immediate effect on Shell's stock price, which was trading in the high $60s at the time, and then climbed to $75 in October. But when Shell lost half its stake in December, the effects started showing. The Sakhalin project was expected to provide a significant share of Shell's reserves, and it was especially important because Shell's other reserves were starting to look a bit doubtful. So it's no surprise that investors reacted. The stock, which was trading above $70, was at $66 by mid-January 2007, and down to $64 by the end of February 2007.

Now as an investor, there's no way you could really know that Putin was going to pull this power play. But you can be alert to the news. I would have sold in December, as soon as the news of Putin's move broke; that way I would have taken some loss, but probably saved myself $4 a share. The lesson is clear: The foreign markets for natural resources are extremely unpredictable, and this can profoundly affect companies. So if you're looking to dabble in companies that are dependent on unreliable regimes, be prepared for bad news, and respond accordingly. Be careful, though! Shell's stock has since rebounded with the rising price of oil and, with Shell's massive size and scale, we see that "news" can often be overshadowed, ultimately, by other factors. But grab the trade while "news" is brewing or fresh!

If you're a risk-averse investor, you may want to stay out of emerging markets completely. Many of the truly emerging markets (like Africa and South America) represent big-wave surfing, but some (like China and India) may represent excellent investments, depending on the industry. A good rule of thumb here is checking out how much business American and other multinational corporations are deriving from a particular emerging market. Most multinational companies already have some presence in China, and many are beginning to see substantial profits from the region. When BlackBerry owner Research In Motion was close to receiving an entry permit to sell in China, the stock rose more than 20 percent in two trading days. So China would be a safer investment than, say, northern Africa, where few multinational companies have thriving businesses.

One smart way to diversify your portfolio in order to have some emerging-markets benefit is to invest in mutual funds specializing in a single emerging market (China or India, for example) or a broad spectrum of emerging markets. By leaving the decisions to fund analysts who know much more about these regions than you do, you can expose yourself to the upside while exposing yourself to less risk. But even these funds do carry risk, so make sure you research them as carefully as you would a stock.

The Rise of the Megacity

In 1950, Greater New York and London were the world's only "megacities," that is, urban areas with populations of more than 10 million. There were nine such cities in 1985, nineteen in 2004—and twenty-five in 2005! The rise of these megacities is one of the most important international trends of the twenty-first century, and as the jump from 2004 to 2005 would suggest, it's only accelerating. Whether it's Mexico City (24 million), Seoul (23 million), or Mumbai (formerly Bombay, 21 million), these population centers are growing rapidly around the globe, and they are creating enormous strains in terms of infrastructure, employment, poverty, housing, crime, and just about everything else.

As nations attempt to address the many issues raised by rapid population growth, there will be tremendous opportunities for corporations that offer solutions. Like anything else with emerging markets, there is great opportunity along with the risk for investors who want to get in on this extraordinarily important trend.

Many of these companies will be focusing on infrastructure, which is so essential to a city's well-being. One such company is Companhia de Saneamento Basico, which is the sole provider of water and sewage services for the Sao Paulo region of Brazil, a rapidly growing area that currently has 22.3 million people. The Brazilian government is the largest shareholder, and it has been allowing SBS to raise its fees at rates higher than inflation, which has kept the profits rolling in. With a service that is in constant demand, and with room for growth (as of this writing, only 78 percent of the population had sewerage services), this company's stock has been rising steadily—jumping from about $5 in 2003 to over $30 in early 2007—and I think its future is extremely bright.

Sure, sewerage treatment may be unappealing, and water is certainly not exciting, but they're both essential services, which is why Companhia de Saneamento Basico has been trending steadily upward and will likely keep rising. A company like this certainly has some risks. For one thing, the interests of the Brazilian government may not always be in the interests of minority stakeholders around the world—an issue facing any investor who wants to be a part of the megacity expansion. Most such companies will be extremely reliant on government policy, which will generally be geared to the concerns of the populace rather than the bottom line. As with any emerging economy, a recession could significantly curtail government tax receipts and thus the support for capital investments necessary to infrastructure growth. Fortunately in the case of Companhia de Saneamento Basico, the highly regarded Luiz Inácio Lula da Silva is in charge in Brazil and has been managing the country with a steady hand. Best of all, this is a stock that trades on the New York Stock Exchange, so you don't have to mess around on any foreign exchanges to buy it!

For investors who want to make money on companies like Companhia de Saneamento Basico, do your research and find the cities that are growing most rapidly. Look into companies that are deeply involved in the basic growth of the cities, or look for mutual funds that focus on emerging markets and especially on the countries with the cities that interest you. But as you're doing your research into the cities, make sure you get a sense of their national leadership as well.

Who's In Charge?

An important tip for investing in the world economies is to make sure you're investing in leadership. Just as I will follow Sam Zell wherever his brilliant mind takes him, you can look to leaders who are taking their countries forward, and focus your investments on their nations. I've already discussed how many leaders are willing to put their own interests ahead of those of their citizens, and corporations are much less willing to get involved in a nation with bad leadership. But there are also leaders who are doing the right thing and taking their countries forward.

As of this writing, leaders moving in the right direction to watch in Latin America are Lula in Brazil and Michel Bachelet in Chile. Both are moderates who are leading their countries to economic prosperity. In Africa, a man like Olusegun Obsanjo has helped Nigeria recover from decades of military dictatorship. Although there are questions about corruption in his administration and about his dedication to democracy and the smooth transfer of power, he appears to be much better for the country's economic and social well-being than someone like Robert Mugabe of Zimbabwe, who has sunk his country into a tragic morass of poverty and violence. The potential stock market winners in the global arena can be found long before these countries enjoy surging stock economies. Watch the news for hints about what's to come down the road.

At the same time, remember that an open society isn't

everything for a country's success. Look at China, for example, or the extremely rigid government in Singapore that has managed a very successful economy. In Central Asia, you can look at Nursultan Nazarbayev, who has cracked down on dissent but successfully managed Kazakhstan's economy and petroleum and natural gas resources to create stable growth for his country. There's still far too much poverty, but there's also hope that Kazakhstan's natural resources and shrewd management will lead to steady growth in years to come. Compared with Nazarbayev, the late Saparmurat Niyazov doesn't come out too well. Turkmenistan enjoys the fourth largest natural gas reserves in the world, along with plenty of oil, but poor leadership has resulted in ridiculously high unemployment and frequent shortages of electricity and water.

Of course much is unpredictable in emerging markets, and as I've mentioned, you may feel safer going through mutual funds, or through American companies that are investing abroad. One thing is for sure, though. To be a good detective, you have to not only pay attention to what's happening in our own backyard, but also understand what's happening in other places. That company in China may be onto the next big alternative-energy source, and even if we decide to invest only in the United States, our investments will still be impacted by those developments. Always pay attention to global news and apply what you learn to your investments.

TREND TIP 8

In Your Wildest Imagination . . .

The Role of Creativity in Spotting Trends

If you could invent anything in the world, what would it be? Curiosity does not kill the cat when it comes to making money. The best entrepreneurs in this world use their imaginations, and when you do the same, you can identify the trends worth investing in. I like to consider this trend exercise as being akin to the Six Degrees game. Imagine something that we need or something we want. What do you wish you could have, if you could have anything in the world? What do you crave? What would make your life easier? Thinking this way can lead you to obvious answers and to some less obvious answers—and they can help you identify trends before they even start.

Just as you don't need to be a mathematical genius to study the stats that can help you invest, you don't need to be a massively creative person to use your imagination in this way. The other morning, I got together with a financially struggling (and I might add, rather high-strung) friend of mine at Starbucks. As I was stirring sugar into my latte, and rather presumptuously giving her pointers on how she might get out of debt, she suddenly blurted out, "But you're so lucky! Everything you touch turns to gold." She proceeded to tell me that I clearly was born to make money, while she was born to lose it.

I assured my friend that she was wrong: First of all, I've invested in my fair share of big duds along the line. Second of all, *no one* is born to get rich or born to be poor. We all have an equal shot at making money from the market.

"Be a dreamer," I told my friend.

She scoffed, "With the amount of time I spend dreaming of making money, I should have been filthy rich a long time ago!" I explained that I didn't mean dreaming about *money*. We all do that, usually in the context of worrying. What I meant was thinking about *the everyday world* in a different way. *Imagination can open your eyes wide to the opportunity all around you at any given moment*—and can allow you to cash in at the end of the day. With imagination, you can sometimes jump on trends before they are officially trends, especially if you keep your imagination ticking while you are running errands, reading the newspaper, taking the kids to school, attending work meetings; all the time.

I pointed to the Starbucks cup in her hand by way of example. "Take Howard Schultz, the genius behind Starbucks," I said. "You might think it doesn't take imagination to start a coffee shop, but take it a few steps further, as Schultz did, and you are onto something." In the '80s and early '90s, Schultz saw that Americans were always on the go and they desperately wanted two things. One, they sought an affordable indulgence that would feel like a reward for their stressful lives. Even a $4 latte is cheap enough for many people to splurge on every day without feeling too guilty. Two, they craved a place to relax. So he provided them with a home away from home where they could indulge themselves. It was so simple: he saw a market hole and created a way to fill it. His creativity plus execution led to innovation, which is the hallmark of companies that can develop or capitalize on trends.

You could have capitalized on having the *imagination* and vision of Howard Schultz—by buying stock in his Starbucks! What if you had shared his vision, and bought shares of Starbucks when it first went public in 1992? If you had invested just $1 on that first day, you would have roughly $55 dollars today. If you invested $1,000 on that day, it would be worth around $55,000 today. I'd call that a healthy return.

So you don't need to have a creative writing or fine arts degree to have an imagination for present and future trends. When I'm dreaming, I like to keep several key points in mind.

Where There Is a Problem, There Is Money To Be Made

Our current environmental woes are a good example of this. We have to fix what we've broken, or our planet will be in rough shape. But how do we fix what's broken? Entrepreneurs use their imaginations, and trend spotters keep their eye out for environmentally smart companies and innovations. Ethanol additives, wind power, hybrid cars, solar panels, and other green innovations can equal big business. I know I've mentioned these areas before, but the Green Revolution bears mentioning again and again because I'm confident it will be one of the most substantial trends of the twenty-first century.

I made quite a bit of money by applying an innovation lens to solutions to our environmental problems. Everyone groans about how the price of heating their home has kept rising; heating oil keeps going up, natural gas is keeping pace, and even firewood prices have gotten much higher. In October 2005 a friend who is a contractor was talking about how many people were opting for propane instead of heating oil to save money. I asked why *everyone* wasn't using propane. He explained that, in the past, propane tanks were unattractive (remember what you've learned about human nature in Trend Tip 3!). But I knew there would be a financial tipping point at which people wouldn't care about attractive anymore, if it came to saving money. Plus, you can use propane for your gas range, which in my experience works much better than natural gas for cooking.

Right after our conversation, I started looking for propane companies, and came across Suburban Propane Partners LP; they sell everything from fuel oil to natural gas and other refined fuels, and they install and service heating, ventilation, and air conditioning (HVAC), though the company has announced it will be streamlining these areas to focus more on the core business. Their core business is propane, and because it is a real pain to switch fuel companies—often it involves changing tanks and other equipment—Suburban's customers can be counted on as repeat business.

So there you have it: tackle a problem with your imagination. In this case, the problem was oil prices on the way up. Use just a tiny stretch of the imagination, coupled with other trend tips, like Think Like a Detective, talk to everyone you know, and you'll find an answer; in this case, propane companies stand to prosper. You can't beat a good product with captive customers and increasing demand on the horizon. People told me Suburban was an established company, an institution. Quick research on the company's financials bore out that conclusion. Its dividend yield was close to 10 percent a year. I bought on November 4, 2005, when it was at $24, and have watched it climb to $42 in just over a year. I guess I'm a captive customer now, too!

Watch for Market Holes

Sometimes you might see a small but obvious hole in the market. (Think of the lack of coffee shops where you could relax, in the Howard Schultz/Starbucks' example earlier in this chapter.) If you see the market hole, chances are an entrepreneur has seen the same thing and is working around the clock to launch a service or product to fill it. Your imagination might lead you to simple needs or to wilder ideas. Pizza delivery in trucks outfitted with kitchens, where the pizza is made on the way to delivery so it is piping hot when it arrives? Done! A fee-based rental service like Netflix but with music downloads instead of DVD rentals? Done! Keeping a creative mind will let you act more quickly when one of these products or services enters the marketplace.

Sometimes the market hole is obvious, but how the service fills the void is where the true innovation occurs. For instance, much ado has been made about our inability to save money. Many people are retiring with few resources, yet people are living longer and longer. In came the insurance companies, eager for new opportunities to grow their business. In this case, the new product was longevity insurance. Basically, you buy a longevity policy around retirement age and it provides you with guaranteed lifetime income beginning around age 80 to 85. It is a simple solution to a problem that many elderly people face today, and it is a terrific money-making opportunity for the insurance companies. How can you as an imaginative trend spotter benefit? Again, by having the creative vision to recognize where these market holes exist, and keeping your eyes peeled for imaginative, smart companies offering products and services to fill these holes.

One entrepreneur who has made a fortune off seeing a hole in the market and finding a creative way to fill it is John Mackey, CEO and cofounder of the wildly successful Whole Foods chain of natural foods supermarkets. When he started the company in 1978, he was a college dropout who, to any outside observer, would appear to be a hippie like many of his generation at the time. He lived in a cooperative and wore his hair long. He loved all-natural foods. With his girlfriend, Renee Lawson Hardy, Mackey opened a small vegetarian store in Austin, Texas, called Safer Way Natural Foods. As he and his business partner observed Safer Way's success, they concluded that demand for healthy food and sustainable living practices wasn't going to disappear. This wasn't just a '70s trend. As the number of bigger, mainstream groceries increased, and subsequently the number of mom-and-pop markets dropped, they determined that the desire for homegrown produce and pesticide-free food would likely increase. Yet, in the supermarkets, it was becoming increasingly hard to uncover where the food you were buying was coming from. You had no idea if it was safe or healthy. You could get whatever you wanted for cheaper prices than ever before, but organic and local food was harder and harder to afford, because the health food stores simply didn't have the economies of scale that the massive supermarkets offered.

Why, thought Mackey, couldn't the natural foods industry turn its sights to the supermarket format? Bigger might be better. He approached another natural foods market, in Austin, and the two stores merged to form Whole Foods Market. Located in Austin, the first store had a staff of only nineteen. But Whole Foods was an instant hit and quickly began to grow. In 1992, the chain went public, trading on the NASDAQ under ticker symbol WFMI. At the time of writing this book, Whole Foods Market is an international chain, the world's leading natural and organic foods supermarket, a Fortune 500 company with a market capitalization of nearly $7 billion.

But what was at the root of Whole Foods's astronomical success? Was it simply a matter of John Mackey's seeing that no one else had applied the natural foods market model to the supermarket chain format, and doing it himself? To be sure, that was just part of Whole Foods's success.

Yes, Mackey saw a hole in the market for a supermarket-size natural foods store. But what made him truly visionary was the strength of his imagination: how he filled the market hole. He recognized that the natural foods model would actually *fail* if it directly imitated the big-market format. First and foremost, the whole foods movement is a *culture*. And the whole culture surrounding the organic foods consumer doesn't jibe with the corporate, cold, and capitalistic feel of a traditional supermarket—even if that market sold organic turnips and free-range eggs. The model of the supermarket business is cost cutting; and for most chains, that includes minimizing pay to employees, selling produce of lesser quality, and basically doing whatever else it takes to make a buck. Supermarkets are generally unfriendly places: employees aren't particularly happy to be working there, the stores are often messy and hard to navigate, and shopping is typically an unpleasant chore.

So Mackey set out to make a supermarket that provided a shopping experience in line with the feel of a local health food store—where shoppers and employees alike tend to be conscious of working standards, healthy environments, and happy people. And yet, the store would still be able to succeed financially on the level of a traditional supermarket. And he did. Not only did he and his partners create a store where the products were top quality, they created a working culture that feels egalitarian. At Whole Foods, executives have a pay cap and their salary information is open to all employees.

And you, as a trend spotter following Trend Tip 8, can have a similar active imagination. I'll say it again and again: it is not rocket science. Mackey saw there was a way to turn the small, expensive health food market into a supermarket in terms of economy of scale, without sacrificing the wholesome, feel-good quality surrounding the healthy-living culture. If you saw this market hole, and had your eyes peeled for innovative solutions to fill the hole, you would have spied Whole Foods early in the game and had the chance to make plenty of money from it. And applying your innovation lens to check if this phenomenon was satisfying a real need in the marketplace helps you distinguish between lasting trends and all the hype.

Use Your Imagination in the Fast-Changing Tech World

Communication needs drive trends, and vice versa. Humans have always relied on one person communicating with another—whether it was by smoke signal, pony express, cell phone, or the internet. The last few years, technology has made huge progress in enabling people to communicate. As I mentioned earlier, I made quite a bit of money off this trend by investing in Webex, eBay, and even Apple right before they made their big announcement of the Apple iPhone, but it won't stop there. What is the next trend? Use your imagination, and couple it with some research. Look to earlier tips, like Trend Tip 6, Study the Stats, to find such trend indicators as demographic shifts, then determine, using the help of Trend Tip 1, Play the Six Degrees of Making Bacon, how these trend shifts might possibly impact the world.

Don't limit your mind—you'll be surprised what you might come up with. Usually, if you imagine it, someone in big business has already imagined it as well. The advantage is that you will be well ahead of the curve. You will be able to keep your eyes peeled for when that special investment opportunity presents itself and capitalize on it.

Let's take an example of something going forward: our workforce. As I've noted before, we're facing an increased labor shortage heading into the next decade. But other labor shifts are occurring as well. As technology gets more advanced, it has become increasingly easy to have a mobile workforce. I know at least ten friends employed by major New York City corporations and businesses who work from home at least one day a week—usually Friday! And they all say they actually get more work done outside the office, without the distraction of colleagues and the interruptions of pointless meetings upon meetings, than they do on Monday through Thursday. According to the Sulzer Infrastructure Network, a London-based consulting firm, by 2010 at least half the American labor force will be working two or more days outside the formal office space. Take this statistic and run with it in your imagination. You likely can see how it will manifest itself in many ways, particularly in technology. Telecommuting is going to become more and more common, which means that any company that deals in network infrastructure will likely get a big boost. At the same time, demand for office space may decline, and companies that focus on office real estate in major metropolitan areas may take a hit.

Telecommunications will keep advancing. If we are all connected today through a modem and high-speed internet, along with our cell phones and Treos and BlackBerries, I can only imagine what the world may look like five or ten years down the line. I'm going to keep my eye on integrated technology. Just as the lines between office and home are melting, I'll not be shocked if we are just steps from work and home being fully integrated: the TV, computer, refrigerator, phone, office fax, coffeemaker, video conferencing, and radio will all be part of the same small device. And further along, why not imagine chips in the brain that enable us to talk to our colleagues without having to speak!

While this tip may lead you to create scenarios that seem more like a science fiction movie than a money-making trend, the exercise can help you keep your mind open to the possibilities of technological invention, so that when you see that special thing actually invented, you will understand how it will—or won't, as the case may be—revolutionize the world. You will know when to ride the wave to the bank, or sit back and wait for a better one to roll along.

A robot is my barber. Innovations are endless. Read the science journals as well as the business journals, to stay abreast of what might be coming down the road. Dolly the sheep is only the beginning. Cloned food sources, robotic hairdressers, tracking chips to put on children . . . While there are some complicated moral implications linked to much of this technology, the research is all being driven by the promise of riches at the other end.

What about demographics: the aging baby boomers? As we live longer and longer, what innovations will come about to satisfy our needs? We will want to live at home or some place else comfortable—anything but being dumped in a nursing home. What innovations will we see to satisfy this demand? Certainly, there is going to be a rise in deluxe retirement communities. But take a look at other demographics as well. There is a serious shortage of nurses, but demand for home health care is on the rise. Will medical care be outsourced in some way? Will we see technology step in? Your innovation radar can help you search out new companies (or new business lines of existing companies) that are currently poised to capture the future trends before they become trends, helping you to buy low.

Don't Get Too Carried Away

While employing Trend Tip 8, you have to be wary that some innovation is simply too innovative. Sometimes the innovation isn't all that practical (think of the Segway example mentioned earlier). And while people like new things, sometimes it takes them time to get accustomed. An example: Americans—and, increasingly, people abroad—are *always* looking for ways to simplify their lives, to make chores take less time. My imagination is always open to new innovations that may offer speed—whether it be new internet applications or improved vacuum cleaners. These tend to be quickly adopted by the market, and can provide windfalls to investors. The iRobot vacuum is an example. When it was released in 2002, I thought, *This is a brilliant concept.* I hate to vacuum—and suddenly, for not much money, I can buy this cute little machine that looks like a miniature UFO and zips around doing the vacuuming for me. It can even get at the hard-to-reach spots under the sofa and beds. The concept and the design is pure genius.

I not only bought an iRobot vacuum, I flagged the start-up company as one to watch. When it went public in 2005, it was a disappointment. It opened at $24 and climbed for a few months, but it was below its IPO price within a year and has only briefly touched $24 again since then; as of this writing it's below $15. Not every stock that is based on a genius, inventive product will be recognized right away by the marketplace. I got in cheap at $16. And I will hang onto this stock, because I think the company is doing things in the right way, has more inventive products around the corner, and is run by the visionary technologist Rodney Brooks, who is sure to have more tricks up his sleeve.

Along these same lines, sometimes "old-fashioned" technologies and products work just fine: can you really build a better mousetrap? When you're using your imagination, don't forget to compare the new with the old. Look not just at new technologies and ideas but also at traditional technologies and methodologies that are being improved on a daily basis, and are trusted. Western Union is a company that has been doing their core business well and as a market leader since 1851. After an earlier merger with First Data, it was spun off in 2006. Western Union is still the only game in town as individuals and businesses start to spread out globally but still need to transfer money in one efficient and recognized manner that is considered trustworthy and technologically safe. Demographics and globalization meet old-fashioned trustworthiness. I have just invested, and I am betting that Western Union's stock performs well over the next five years. But of course, I will be watching to see if any competitors, like the big banks, start to nip in any meaningful way at Western Union's heels. (Remember, part of the success of investing is knowing when to sell and never falling in love with a stock—instead fall in love with the trend-watching game!)

I love Trend Tip 8, because I love to use my imagination. What in your wildest imagination can you come up with as a future solution to a long-term problem? If you can imagine it today, no question a business will imagine it—and implement it tomorrow. If the idea is as good as it seems to be, this company will profit, and so will you. Sometimes you have to be patient while the rest of the world catches up with the idea, and sometimes you need to come back down to earth and realize that some ideas are simply not feasible or practical to ever take off in a big way.

If you want to take using your imagination one step further—and you are the ambitious type—there is no reason you can't implement a novel, great idea yourself. Hey, one of the best things I've done in my life is to start my own business. Nothing—short of having my lovely daughter—has been as rewarding. By spotting trends with the idea of jumping on stock opportunities, sometimes you might hit on an idea that is simply too good not to pursue yourself. That's the biggest wave of all to surf. It is high-risk, but if it succeeds, it will be the best—and most lucrative—ride of your life!

TREND TIP 9

To Every Trend There Is an Equal and Opposite Trend

Power in Going Against the Flow

So you've bought this book to read nine tips about spying and riding trends, only to find that the very last tip of the book, Trend Tip 9, tells you, *Don't follow trends!* What?! Before you throw this book across the room or go back to the store for a refund, hear me out.

At the end of his famous poem "The Road Not Taken," Robert Frost claims that taking the less popular road "has made all the difference." As antithetical as it may seem, Frost's point is something always to keep in mind: he or she who takes the path less traveled may make more money in the long run. Only instead of taking a road, in trend spotting sometimes you should be riding a different wave. Imagine that you are waiting out there on the open ocean with everyone else. A good-looking wave comes along—it is obviously strong—and everyone else rides it in. Their ride isn't as satisfying as they hoped; for one thing, there are too many other people on the wave to make it worthwhile.

You instead wait it out. You opt for an unusual wave. Maybe it doesn't look as hot to others, but you see something in the way it is curling—and you take a risk that it will pay off. Or maybe it simply looks like a fine wave, not big but stable, and you jump on it. With a nod to Robert Frost, if you take the wave less surfed, it can make a huge financial difference.

The point of Trend Tip 9 is that, at times, it's okay to jump on something that isn't trendy. And likewise, it's occasionally more prudent to play it safe, treading water in the kiddy pool with solid stocks, while the rest of your friends are out there high-risk surfing. Sure, it's fun and lucrative to surf, but sometimes it can be painful. Sometimes the ride doesn't last and you wipe out. Sometimes the wave is too crowded and no one wins. As with everything, I go for the moderate approach. As I said in the introduction, I believe in taking the middle ground. Sometimes I'll drop in on a huge wave, take the risk, and have it pay off. But at other times I'm just as content riding a smaller wave, or even—as this chapter will describe in more detail—treading water in the kiddy pool. There is money to be made in playing it safe or going against the tide.

Sometimes a trend creates a negative opportunity. It is important to understand this when all the analysts and financial gurus are yelling "Jump"—sometimes you should do just the opposite.

Strong Brands Aren't Trendy

It is worth remembering that not everything profitable comes in the form of a trend. Certain products and services don't have peaks and valleys that coincide with the public's whims. Certain things are dependable winners—they are not hot, never "up," but they also are never cold or "down." Take Johnson & Johnson, as a perfect example. What could possibly be less interesting than a company that makes Listerine, Tylenol, and Pepcid AC? This behemoth pharmaceutical, consumer goods, and medical devices company has been around forever, it seems, and everyone knows it. That it is a solid company is no secret, so how can you profit from it? You aren't discovering anything new. But when you think about the fact that these products, however boring, are in daily use by millions of people around the world, Johnson & Johnson suddenly doesn't seem quite so unattractive. They pour great resources into research and development and, as such, are committed to continue growing the company and producing new and profitable products. And not surprisingly, its stock price has been similarly appealing. Sure, it's had its ups and downs, but the stock has always come back from its dips; sometimes it takes a little while, but this is a stock to hold for the long term for its steady growth and the small dividend.

There doesn't seem to be a role for solid, big brands in the world of trend surfing. As I said, strong brands are not trendy. While riding them may not be thrilling, it certainly can provide you with more profit than investing the same money in a traditional bank account. They are slow, steady waves, but they rarely crash against the rocks, rarely fizzle to nothing. For example, during the tail end of the internet boom of the late nineties, investing in strong branded blue chip stocks wasn't trendy, but it would have prevented a lot of investors from wiping out on dot-com stocks. Sometimes the safe surfer is the surfer who is having the most success—and can be relaxed about it in the process.

Anti-Trends Are Cool

One of the reasons investing in anti-trends can be profitable is that these things often turn into trends with time. Take, for instance, skateboarding, the ultimate antiestablishment activity. It eventually became so cool to be against the mainstream that skateboarding became mainstream. Everyone wanted to get in on it—they wanted to be different, hip, edgy. And now skateboarding is big business. Tony Hawk is a household name.

Sometimes one trend set in motion suggests that an

opposite trend will happen later. A few years ago, the Atkins craze had many people forgoing starch. Most analysts rightfully predicted that companies producing bread products would suffer. If you were a trend spotter, you'd likely have pulled your money from companies that sold starchy foods. And in many cases, that would have been a good move.

But during this time, I got to know the chain Panera Bread. Anytime I went into one of their stores, it was packed. And their bread was absolutely scrumptious. So despite the trend away from bread, I bought shares in Panera in March 2001 at $11.50. By mid-March the year following, Panera was up to $31.60 per share, and by mid-March of 2006, it had soared all the way up to $73.63. Part of the lesson learned here is that *sometimes a trend doesn't have the power to influence a valuable brand with an amazing product or service.*

The Unpopular Stepsister Can Sometimes Make You Rich

While the crowd jumps on stocks that are riding trends and feel good to own, you can spot companies that are being overlooked and present excellent value. Right now, I couldn't be a bigger proponent of environmentally conscious, green stocks. At the same time, I understand why someone might want to invest in unclean energy sources. While I would *never* say that an environmentally detrimental product is *cool,* I will sometimes say that the stock that bucks the trend, the company that could care less how trendy it is, can make you a buck.

Take public perception at the time of writing this book. While everyone was jumping into ethanol stocks, I was also buying undervalued oil service companies—the ones that help the traditional fossil fuel companies. Adding another degree to that anti-trend, I was also buying the steel tubing companies that provide the tools for more efficient extraction of crude oil. Now, I would be hard pressed to find anyone who would admit that coal energy is a good thing. It is a pollutant of the highest order. Clearly, clean gas is the way to go. But if you look at more-cutting-edge research on coal, you'll find it's also a lot cheaper and much more plentiful than gas, and that coal use has been rising steadily over the years. Moreover, there are exciting new technologies that may make it possible to burn coal in a much cleaner way, such as carbon capture and sequestration (taking the CO_2 from coal and storing it underground where it can't act as a greenhouse gas). Overall supply and demand numbers tell us that energy demand greatly exceeds any energy amount that can be produced using alternative energy (to say nothing of how many forms of alternative energy such as corn ethanol might fare in the open market if subsidies were eliminated). Coal is still one of the cheapest forms of energy, and still a primary requirement for energy consumption in places like China, where the demand for energy seems insatiable.

And then there's nuclear energy, which has been reviled

ever since the accident at Three Mile Island. Right now, it's quietly making a comeback as perhaps the least damaging of the alternatives. Even many scientists and activists formerly opposed to nuclear energy have decided its advantage—cheap, relatively clean energy—may outweigh the risk of leaking nuclear waste. There's by no means unanimity on this subject, of course, but there's no question nuclear energy is getting a second look.

I'm not suggesting you run out and buy stocks in coal companies or nuclear companies, particularly if you are not in support of their technologies. But I am strongly suggesting that you *be willing to question your assumptions and those of your friends about a company or a trend.* Take the time to find out whether a company, industry, or technology is as bad as everyone says. If you can get ahead of public opinion that may soon shift, you stand to make good money.

The reasons for a company or industry getting a bad rap are numerous, and oftentimes founded on solid data. However, sometimes the assessment is founded simply on public perception and not on fundamentals. As we saw earlier, Halliburton (HAL) is another example of an unpopular stock being a great buy. The challenges to Halliburton seemed to start as soon as Dick Cheney, the former CEO of the behemoth oil services company, took over as vice president of our country. They've continued up to the present. To be sure, there may be something a little unattractive (but probably unavoidable) about the close connections between high-level government officials and a company dependent on government contracts, and there seems to be evidence that Halliburton or its subsidiaries have been overcharging the government for services in Iraq. But the vitriol directed at this company has done nothing to stop its stock from climbing. Its success offers an important lesson to investors: If you have personal problems with investing in a company that makes money off war, you shouldn't invest in a stock like Halliburton. But if you don't have those personal qualms, you may be able to invest for good returns.

If you'd bought Halliburton back in early 2003, as America was gearing up for war with Iraq, you would have paid $10 per share. The price reached $40 in January 2006 and is still above $30 at the time of this writing. Political and moral questions aside, this was clearly a great investment for those who got in at the right time. As you may recall, I made a similar point about how even antidemocratic leaders can be good for their nations' economies. Meanwhile, many so-called socially responsible investment choices aren't squeaky clean. My point is that the lines are unclear, and only you can decide what you're comfortable with.

Key to remember with this subpoint about the ugly stepsister is that, when you invest, you have to live with yourself. I am only partly joking. Do think about investing responsibly. Although making money is an overall goal pushed by this book, as an investor *I personally think it is crucial to be responsible with where you put your money.* Making money is secondary to making the world a better place. So if you don't, for instance, have a problem with coal-burning power plants, by all means try to profit off them. I know that I have trouble compromising some of my strongest held beliefs. Sometimes it simply isn't worth it. *Be conscious of where you put your money. I've been able to sleep at night* and *make money*, and this makes all the difference.

Spotting Where Lemons Might Turn to Lemonade

When a trend negatively affects a company, the trend can sometimes be turned on its head to make money. Think of the trends involving the major accounting scandals of the early twenty-first century. People were highly suspicious of big corporations, particularly following the Enron story of corruption and collapse. And investors' suspicions were not unfounded. Look at a company like Tyco International, the major industrial manufacturer. In 2002, the company was rocked by scandal when former CEO Dennis Kozlowski was arrested for tax evasion and the public learned that he had effectively looted Tyco of over $135 million (this in addition to having earned in three years a salary of $332 million). Included in his corporate spending—all undisclosed to shareholders, of course—was a $6,000 shower curtain. The media jumped on the story. A shower curtain that cost as much as a car, practically! Not surprisingly, after the news of Kozlowski's fraud and the gold shower curtain purchase, the stock plummeted to $15. This was a stock that at one point was flying as high as $60. Corporate corruption aside, a little research showed that it was a solid company with good financials and market position.

This is when I jumped in. In June 2002, I bought Tyco at $15. I knew that the price was temporarily low. Once the scandal blew over, the company would regain its name. Its business could survive this type of scandal—after all, it all revolved around one corrupt man who was no longer part of the company. After I purchased the stock, it sank below $10 within weeks. I realized that I had bought a bit prematurely, but still at a bargain basement price. Sure enough, in February 2004, I sold my shares of Tyco at $28.

The point to remember is that sometimes a trend will adversely affect a company, but if that company is solid in the right ways, most likely the hit it takes will only be temporary. The Tyco example highlights again how doing your homework on the company can help distinguish between reality and (this time, negative) hype.

Crystal Balls Can Be Fragile

Don't pay too much heed to futurists. It is easy to read what all the analysts are predicting and ride every hot trend wave they spy for you. Although taking their advice into account is always prudent, weigh it against everything you know: things you've observed in Nancy Drew / Magnum PI mode, past trends you've noticed, human behavior, and all the other tips in this book.

As I mentioned in Trend Tip 5, it is important to be

aware of what the business pages tell you and what all the analysts tell you. But I like to say to my friends, Don't trust your broker! He or she may have a fancy business school degree, but this doesn't mean the broker knows more than you do. I have spent a lifetime acting on my instincts, and my instincts are rooted in the fundamentals found in this book. By understanding the basics of spying trends, you can keep your eyes open to the opportunity all around you, all the time. You can uncover wonderful new companies, opportunities in old companies, and trends that may, in the future, become grounds for inventions. And you will know when to jump on the wave, invest in these opportunities, and make money.

So after Tips 1–8, telling you how to jump on trends, here in Tip 9 is why you also can stand to profit by going against the trends. Whether it is bucking a trend predicted by the pundits on the financial pages and TV shows, or jumping on a company with solid financials and growth but that is out of favor because of public perception, or playing it safe and putting some money into the tried-but-true big cap, nontrendy companies, there is always money to be made by *not* riding the fast trend wave.

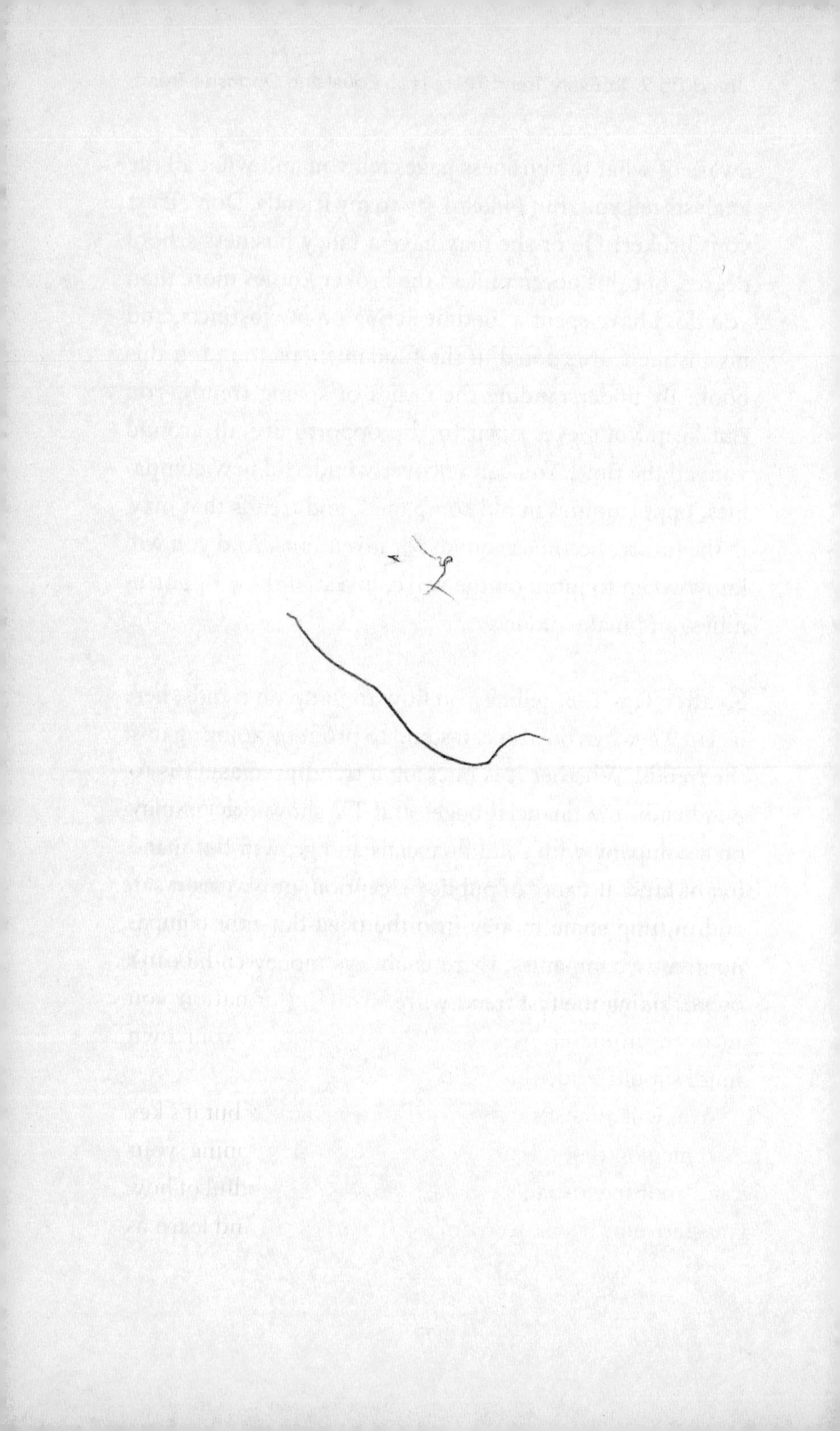

CONCLUSION

Trend Surfing Is Fun

I hope that you have a sense of not only how easy it is to spot trends but also how much fun it can be. You get to play games, draw diagrams, be creative, exercise your mind, and dream. And at the end of the day, you can make money.

Always remember to do your homework on the companies you uncover as possible beneficiaries of a trend. I can't stress this enough. Armed with all the information you uncover, ultimately you still have to make up your own mind: should I ride this wave or not?

You will almost surely make some bad calls, but it's key to remember: don't be hard on yourself. Honing your trend-spotting instincts can take time. So be mindful of how you start out. It's perfectly okay to start small and learn as

I have, from making mistakes. When I jump on a wave and it turns out to be a bad one and I lose some money, I try not to beat myself up. Instead, I analyze what happened and try to discover if I could have predicted the situation any better. Usually, I will take away a powerful lesson that later will help me make money.

After some practice, and some mistakes, you'll find that you're more and more comfortable acting on your instincts. You will spy trends more and more readily. You'll find that you can outperform even the savviest, most educated broker in the field. It just takes patience, some learning, always a bit of luck, and an open mind to ride a solid trend all the way to the bank.

I love surfing, and will do so for the rest of my career. For me, trend spotting has proven to be a lucrative, and thrilling, ride. It keeps me attuned to everything that is going on around me at all times. It encourages me to talk to everyone and, in doing so, not only do I learn many new trend-related things, I also make new friends and expand my horizons. Life is never boring, and it's always full of promise. Every day, in its own way, is like a game. Sure, sometimes I make mistakes and ride waves that wash out. But I know that, if I paddle back out to sea, there will be another great wave to ride soon enough.

I hope this book has helped instill in you some of the basic, creative and fun ways that will help you be a trend spotter and surfer, too. And I hope that, at the end of the day, it will make investing in companies a simple and exciting game for you—and a profitable one, too. Surf's up!

APPENDIX A

Information Resources

General Financial Information Sites

Financial news, industry information, and company-specific news and financial information is available at a number of easy-to-use websites. You will find additional useful information, such as basic growth rate information, financial ratios, P/E information, summary financials, insider transactions, competitor comparisons, and analyst ratings.

Yahoo! Finance	www.finance.yahoo.com
Google Finance	www.finance.google.com
Bloomberg	www.bloomberg.com

Company Filing Information

Publicly traded companies are required to submit regular (quarterly, annual, and major event reports) to the SEC (www.sec.gov/edgar.shtml). The site provides a description of the different types of forms filed by companies (for example, annual report: 10-K; quarterly report: 10-Q, public stock offerings: S-1).

Investment and Business Terminology

Investopedia	www.investopedia.com

Venture Capital and Technology Information

VentureBlog and Red Herring cover both venture capital and the tech trends that VCs follow. *San Jose Mercury News* and the *Seattle Times* are newspapers whose business and technology sections give good insight into what trends VCs follow. The website CNET is a good information source for new tech companies, gadgets, and trends.

VentureBlog	www.ventureblog.com
Red Herring	www.redherring.com
San Jose Mercury News	www.mercurynews.com
Seattle Times	www.seattletimes.nwsource.com
CNET	www.cnet.com

Statistics

FedStats is an easily navigable site summarizing data from various government agencies, sorted by topic. USA.gov and the U.S. Census Bureau sites have a ton of raw data, but they tend to be a bit more cumbersome.

FedStats	www.fedstats.gov
USA.gov	www.usa.gov/Topics/Reference_Shelf/Data.shtml
U.S. Census Bureau	www.census.gov

APPENDIX B

Sample Financial Statements

Appendix B

ACME, Inc.
CONSOLIDATED FINANCIAL STATEMENTS
for the Period Ended December 31, 2006
(In millions of USD)

BALANCE SHEET	12/31/2006	12/31/2005
ASSETS		
Current Assets:		
Cash and Equivalents	$1,510.7	$1,526.2
Short-term Investments	445.3	431.5
Accounts Receivable, Net	2,622.5	2,455.6
Inventories, Net	2,284.4	2,143.7
Other Receivables	163.5	112.4
Deferred Income Taxes	76.1	65.2
Prepaid Expenses and Other Current Assets	270.3	268.5
Total Current Assets	**7,372.8**	**7,003.1**
Property, Plant and Equipment	3,925.1	3,823.4
Less Accumulated Depreciation	1,931.4	1,874.5
Property, Plant and Equipment, Net	**1,993.7**	**1,948.9**
Goodwill	131.5	143.5
Other Assets	452.6	436.2
TOTAL ASSETS	**$9,950.6**	**$9,531.7**
LIABILITIES AND SHAREHOLDERS' EQUITY		
Current Liabilities:		
Line of Credit	$137.4	$125.3
Accounts Payable	1,312.8	1,218.7
Current Portion of Long-term Debt	76.4	74.5
Notes Payable	83.7	83.7
Income Taxes Payable	73.1	67.5
Accrued Liabilities and Other Current Liabilities	135.2	131.5
Total Current Liabilities	**1,818.6**	**1,701.2**
Long-term Liabilities:		
Long-term Debt, Net of Current Portion	353.1	425.3
Deferred Income Taxes and Other Liabilities	468.2	451.8
Total Long-term Liabilities	**821.3**	**877.1**
Shareholders' Equity:		
Additional Paid-in Capital	250.0	250.0
Retained Earnings	2,815.6	2,458.3
Shareholders' Equity	4,245.1	4,245.1
Total Shareholders' Equity	**7,310.7**	**6,953.4**
TOTAL LIABILITIES AND SHAREHOLDERS' EQUITY	**$9,950.6**	**$9,531.7**

Appendix B

ACME, Inc.
CONSOLIDATED FINANCIAL STATEMENTS
for the Period Ended December 31, 2006
(In millions, except per share data)

INCOME STATEMENT	Twelve Months Ended 12/31/2006	% Sales	12/31/2005	% Sales	Y-on-Y % Chg
Revenues	**$4,636.8**	100%	**$4,223.4**	100%	*10%*
Cost of Goods Sold	2,456.1	53%	2,311.2	55%	*6%*
Gross Profit	**1,735.2**	37%	**1,574.1**	37%	*10%*
Operating Expenses:					
Sales & Marketing	958.1	21%	811.6	19%	*18%*
General and Administrative Expense	234.7	5%	212.9	5%	10%
Total Operating Expenses	**1,190.8**		**1,024.5**		
Operating Income	**544.4**	12%	**549.6**	13%	*–1%*
Interest Income (Expense), Net	(16.1)	0%	(9.2)	0%	*75%*
Other Income, Net	10.8	0%	13.5	0%	*–20%*
Income before Provision for Income Taxes	**549.7**	12%	**545.3**	13%	*1%*
Provision for Income Taxes	192.4	4%	190.9	5%	*1%*
NET INCOME	**$357.3**	8%	**$354.4**	8%	*1%*
Diluted EPS	$1.59		$1.58		*10%*
Basic EPS	$1.63		$1.62		*10%*
Weighted Average Common Shares Outstanding:					
Diluted	225.0		225.0		
Basic	219.0		219.0		

Appendix B

ACME, Inc.
CONSOLIDATED FINANCIAL STATEMENTS
for the Period Ended December 31, 2006
(In millions of USD)

STATEMENT OF CASH FLOWS	2006
CASH FLOWS FROM OPERATING ACTIVITIES:	
Net Income	$357.3
Adjustments to Reconcile Net Income to Net Cash Provided by Operating Activities:	
Depreciation and Amortization	68.9
(Increase) Decrease in Accounts Receivable	(166.9)
(Increase) Decrease in Inventories	(140.7)
(Increase) Decrease in Other Receivables	(51.1)
(Increase) Decrease in Deferred Income Taxes	(10.9)
(Increase) Decrease in Prepaid and Other Current Assets	(1.8)
(Increase) Decrease in Accounts Payable	94.1
(Increase) Decrease in Income Taxes Payable	5.6
(Increase) Decrease in Accrued Liabilities and Other Current Liabilities	3.7
Net Cash Provided (Used) by Operating Activities	**158.2**
CASH FLOWS FROM INVESTING ACTIVITIES:	
Acquisitions of Property and Equipment, Net	(89.3)
Other Capital Expenditures	(12.4)
Net Cash Provided (Used) by Investing Activities	**(101.7)**
CASH FLOWS FROM FINANCING ACTIVITIES:	
Proceeds from Borrowing Activities	14.0
Repayments of Bank Borrowings	(72.2)
Dividends Paid	0.0
Repurchase of Common Shares	0.0
Net Cash Provided (Used) by Financing Activities	**(58.2)**
Net Increase (Decrease) in Cash and Cash Equivalents	-1.7
Cash and Cash Equivalents, Beginning of Period	1,957.7
Cash and Cash Equivalents, End of Period	**1,956.0**

Index

Index

About the Author

HILARY KRAMER is a specialist in global investing. Her expertise spans more than twenty years of experience in equity research, asset allocation, and portfolio management. Ms. Kramer's investment track record has led to her becoming known as an industry expert, who is often asked to provide market commentary to *The Wall Street Journal,* ABC, Bloomberg, and CNBC, among others. Ms. Kramer is the finance editor of America Online and also serves as AOL's Money Coach. She appears regularly as a commentator on the *Nightly Business Report* on PBS, providing investment insights.

In 2005, Ms. Kramer founded GreenTech Research LLC, focusing on stocks in such emerging and growing sectors as alternative energy, natural resources, clean technologies, and environmental products and services. Ms. Kramer has held directorships in both NYSE- and NASDAQ-traded companies and, from 1994 to 2002, was the senior managing director of a $5.2 billion global investment fund with both private equity and publicly traded securities.

Hilary Kramer began her career in the investment banking division of Morgan Stanley in 1986. She served as senior strategist for Montgomery Asset Management and worked in Lehman Brothers' structured finance and investment banking divisions.

She served as a Trustee of the Hewitt School, where she managed the endowment, and has sat on the boards of the Colombian American and Venezuelan American Associations. Ms. Kramer is an avid golfer—she was captain of her college's golf team and president of the Wharton School's golf club. From March through May 2003 of the Iraq War, Ms. Kramer was embedded with the U.S. Navy on the USS *Constellation.*

Ms. Kramer received her BA in Latin America Studies from Wellesley College in 1986 and her MBA from the Wharton School at the University of Pennsylvania in 1991.